NOT RELIABLE GUIDES

AN ANALYSIS OF SOME COVENANT COMMUNITY STRUCTURES

ADRIAN J. REIMERS

GARRETT COUNTY PRESS

Not Reliable Guides

An Analysis of Some Covenant Community Structures
by Adrian J. Reimers

Published by
Garrett County Press
931 N Tonti Street
New Orleans, LA 70119

Distributed by Simon & Schuster

ISBN: 978-1-939430-28-1 (paperback)

Library of Congress Control Number: 2026932591

Cover design by Kevin Stone (good-design-is-good.com)

Printed in the United States of America
First Edition: March 2026

PRAISE FOR *NOT RELIABLE GUIDES*

"In Not Reliable Guides, Adrian Reimers provides a perceptive description of parallel Catholic Church structures, such as The People of God, explaining with copious examples how they are not truly parallel, but accepting of Church doctrine and hierarchical structures in some cases and deviating from them in others. Over-all, this is an excellent and well-researched description of para-Church structures."

— NICHOLAS P. CAFARDI, JD, JCD,
Dean Emeritus, Duquesne University School of Law

"The growth of the new Catholic communities is one of the most distinctive of the post-Vatican II period and raises issues that are primarily not political, but theological and ecclesiological: their relationship with the Church and its authorities. This book by Adrian Reimers is one of those books that cannot be dismissed easily by any of the different camps into which the intra-Catholic theological and ecclesial debate is divided today."

—MASSIMO FAGGIOLI, Trinity College Dublin

"A much-needed addition to the wave of writing about charismatic Catholic groups like People of Praise since the confirmation of Amy Coney Barrett to the Supreme Court. In Not Reliable Guides, Adrian Reimers takes on these groups from the inside, writing as a former member with deep knowledge of their history and critiquing them in the language and logic of Catholic ecclesiology. This is an important book, as sympathetic to the people within Catholic charismatic communities as it is unsparing to their ideas."

- Mac Loftin, author of
In the Twilight of the Christian West: A Theology of Mourning and Resistance

"During the time period covered by this book (1960-2025) there have been hundreds of studies of intentional communities, both secular and religious. Almost all, however, have been written from a sociological or psychological perspective, and few, if any, have analyzed Roman Catholic intentional communities. Professor Reimers has therefore done an invaluable service in applying theology and philosophy to his analysis of charismatic covenant communities in the Catholic Church. It provides an important alternative perspective that complements those of the secular sciences."

— Sister Patricia Wittberg, SC,
Emerita Professor of Sociology, Indiana University

"The Second Vatican Council (1962-1965) ushered in changes that left many American Catholics feeling adrift. Some Catholics, seeking stability in an age of chaos, created new 'covenant communities' ostensibly devoted to authentic renewal within the Church. By the 1990s, many of these groups had come under scrutiny for heretical teachings and authoritarian abuse of members. Adrian J. Reimers, a former member of one of these communities, draws on his personal experiences and understanding of Catholic theology to provide a cautionary tale for how movements for renewal within the Church can so easily become schismatic movements against the Church. The high-water mark of covenant communities has passed, but this story remains relevant as many young Catholics today turn to various forms of radical traditionalism in search of a pure Catholicism free from the confusion they attribute to Vatican II."

—Christopher Shannon, associate professor of history at Christendom College and author of *American Pilgrimage: A Historical Journey Through Catholic Life in a New World* (Ignatius, 2022)

For my children Joe, Teresa, Peter, and George

CONTENTS

FOREWORD

Sitting in my office at Notre Dame in May 2017, I was surprised to receive a phone call from a *Washington Post* reporter, asking about the People of Praise. I said that I had not been a member for almost forty years and said "goodbye." A few minutes later a reporter from the *New York Times* called with the same question, but before I could dismiss her, she explained that President Trump's nominee for the Seventh Circuit Court of Appeals, Amy Coney Barrett, was a member of the People of Praise. Naively (just talking to the *Times* cost me some friends) I agreed to a phone interview, which led to a brief mention in the paper. My moment of fame. It turns out that the Wikipedia article on People of Praise mentions me as one critic of the group, and it even mentions an earlier version of this essay. Judge Barrett's subsequent nomination to the Supreme Court in 2020 brought renewed interest in what I might have to say, which was not much. I had been out of the group for thirty-five years, and I had never even met Justice Barrett! However, in the light of the interest stirred up by these presidential nominations, it is opportune and appropriate to offer for publication a second edition of *Not Reliable Guides*.

The germ of this work was conceived in 1992, when several of us former members of charismatic covenant communities decided to prepare a dossier on these groups. The idea was to present this to the American Catholic bishops at their annual winter conference. In fact, the dossier was never completed, and nothing was presented to the bishops. However, word of the project did reach the ears of some bishops. At the time, one leader of the charismatic movement found himself on an elevator with several bishops, one of whom turned to him and asked, "Why don't they just quit?" It was a question worth pursuing. If these covenant communities are so bad, why don't their members just leave? *Not Reliable Guides* began as my own contribution to this effort to inform the bishops and as such constitutes a kind of reflection even for members past and present of groups like these.

In a way, the bishop's question is pertinent today. To some extent, I was answering questions for myself and those close to me. I also hoped to have something to provide at least to my own local bishop. It was clear that something *had* gone wrong. Some of us in South Bend complained about abuses that we had seen, especially abuses against conscience and the intimacy of conjugal and family relationships. In my study, I found that groups like People of Praise and The Word of God[1] were founded on an ecclesiastical heresy, a conception that effectively evacuated the Church of its sacraments and divine structure and replaced them with purely human fellowship led by men with compelling—but not divinely ordained—personalities. Surely this is not good for people, not good for their spiritual lives.

So, why don't they leave?

One answer forty years ago was *fear*, specifically the fear of spiritual dangers in the world outside the community. Members believed that without the 'covering' of the community's leadership, one is vulnerable to the attacks of the Enemy. In 1971, when these communities were first taking shape, the Church was in turmoil liturgically and especially theologically. We were in the middle of what my wife called the "post-Vatican II frang-out." The covenant communities saw themselves as bulwarks at a time when the Church was "weak, confused and divided." To withdraw from the community's spiritual covering was to expose oneself to the wiles of Satan.

This book is written with the situation of Catholics in mind, with the challenges that covenant communities pose to Catholic Christians. Today we see different, but oddly similar, challenges in the Church. The papacy of Pope Francis was often confusing, giving rise to important doctrinal controversies. In response, purportedly orthodox influencers have appeared on social media and in print. The Catholic looking for certainty can find self-assured spokespersons for the truth on Facebook, Instagram, and X, influencers who claim to know what is *really* going on behind the scenes in the Vatican. One can easily find influencers who can explain not only why Pope Francis was a fraud or at least a heretic, but also why Pope John Paul II was doctrinally indifferent, or why Vatican II was a mistake.

Especially relevant for our time is the communities' vision for men. It is no secret that today men are a troubled lot. Young men, in particular, are in a kind of crisis. They do not know who they are or what they should be. As a group, they are less educated than young women and less focused. Young men do not generally see marriage and fatherhood as an option worth pursuing, and therefore they are marrying later than in previous generations. They are hungry for male friendship, even if they don't realize it. As we shall see, the covenant communities did provide for men, giving them a place and a sense of mission. An unmarried man might well be encouraged by his 'head' to begin courting a young woman with an eye to proposing marriage. All men belonged to men's groups that met once a week. A testimony to the importance of these groups in the lives of men is the fact that after leaving the community (a choice often instigated by the wife), many men continue to meet with men from their former men's group. Among the male populace there continues to be a serious need that covenant communities meet.

In a different way, Catholic women face contemporary challenges. Covenant communities regarded feminism as a dangerous challenge for our time. A part of the characteristic reaction of covenant communities to this challenge has reappeared in the phenomenon of the "tradwife," who sees herself in absolute submission to her husband and rejects the notion that women should have a profession or work outside the home. This notion has found Catholic expression in Stephanie Gordon's *Ask Your Husband: A Catholic Guide to Femininity*, which purports to offer a Scripture-based guide to a woman's true vocation. The author and her husband operate a website to provide counter-cultural advice for living an authentically Catholic life. This book and the phenomenon it represents parallel remarkably with some of the principal errors we see in covenant communities concerning women and the marriage relationship.

Charismatic covenant communities were a bad idea at the time, but the problems they were meant to solve were real. Even as these communities fade away, the problems they addressed have not. They are with us even more dangerously than they were then. The charismatic renewal was a movement founded on a personal encounter with Christ through the Holy Spirit. Charismatic covenant communities systematized this encounter. The early charismatics dreamed of a *renewal* of the Church, and the covenant communities tried to create a perfect community of the perfect, as it were. A priest friend once told me that we should always leave space in the back pews of our churches, so that those who are not perfect (or who think they are imperfect) will have a place. In October 2025, the Dicastery for the Laity, Family, and Life opened an investigation of the Emmanuel Community in France. Emmanuel was founded by the saintly Pierre Goursat within the charismatic renewal in France. Certainly, the Emmanuel community is different from those in the United States, but there are concerns arising from the centralization of the community's government, from the inadequate integration of community with parish life, and the insufficient treatment of abuse cases reported within the group.[2] These are parallel problems seen in such groups in the United States, Australia, and elsewhere.

The Church is real and indefectible. We profess to believe in "the one, holy, catholic, and apostolic Church." We have the Scriptures. And whatever one makes of the charismatic renewal movement and its contemporary manifestations, God has promised and has given us the Holy Spirit. This is what we believe.

That was then, as they say, and this is now. My wife and I were dismissed from the People of Praise forty years ago, and now we have almost no contact with it. Today, the People of Praise and the Sword of the Spirit no longer lead the Catholic charismatic renewal, nor are they significant elements in American Christianity. As much as the Church and the world have changed in forty years, much is still the same, and people are looking for answers. This book illustrates some wrong answers from the past. May this understanding help us to find our way going forward. Indeed, this book may well prove useful for Christians who are not Catholic.

"For freedom Christ has set us free." (Galatians 5:1) By baptism and by our consequent faith, we are incorporated into Christ. Each of us has the truth. Christ promises that the truth will make us free (John 8:32). In his landmark encyclical *Veritatis Splendor*, Pope Saint John Paul II makes clear that the freedom is to be in the service of love—the love of God and the love of neighbor.[3] No merely human structure, such as a man-made charismatic community, may lay claim to the Christian's freedom. We belong to Christ.

INTRODUCTION

"Dear Mother Mary, please don't let me be deceived! Pray for me that Satan won't lead me astray." This was my prayer one spring day in 1983. I had begun praying the rosary on my way to work every day, and I knew that I was in trouble. The Vatican Council documents taught that Mary is the model and mother of the Church. The nuns from my grade school had taught that she would crush the serpent. I knew that Satan was testing me. He was doing the one thing that I and the others in my community most feared—trying to separate me from the people of God, from the Body of Christ. I needed help in my time of temptation.

For the previous twelve years, I had belonged to the People of Praise, a covenant community in South Bend, Indiana. In October 1971, I joined about 30 other people in taking a solemn commitment to form a Christian community in which we would find the essential core of our life in the Spirit. Together we would serve each other in all our needs: spiritual, material, and financial.[4] We would obey the Holy Spirit's directions as manifested to us through our leaders. These leaders were holy men of God, respected leaders of the charismatic renewal. A rumor within the community had it that one of them, a theoretical physicist, had even been nominated for a Nobel Prize. We were uniquely blessed.

We understood that the Lord had given us a special call, one almost unique in salvation history. We were to renew true community in the Church and to help restore the unity of all Christians. The Holy Spirit had called us to be a bulwark against evil and a light to the nations. Because of this great work of God's, Satan was enraged and could be expected to attack our community relentlessly. His principal thrust would be against our covenant, that solemn agreement which made us one, an agreement which was the core commitment of our lives. Satan's only hope for victory against the unified of the Body of Christ lay in separating individual members from that body—especially by undermining their mutual commitment and planting suspicions against their leaders.

It was in this context that I was praying my rosary for protection. For close to a year, I had been assailed by "bad thoughts"—temptations to believe that our leaders were leading us astray, that there was something wrong with the People of Praise. I had been outraged when others had attacked our community in the past, but now I was having those doubts myself. I read the documents of Vatican II, expecting to find clarity. Instead, they only raised further questions. What was especially troubling was that the more I prayed these rosaries, begging Our Lady not to let me be deceived, the more I had these awful thoughts. Eventually it became clear to me where the real deception lay.

By the mercy of God, my family and I found ourselves in Rome to work on a priests' retreat in 1984. Far from the People of Praise, I rediscovered a self that had long been submerged; in doing so we regained a family life that had been increasingly absorbed by something else. This rediscovery was an emotional event for me, involving a fundamental change in my life's direction. Within six months I was out of my job with Charismatic Renewal Services, and Marie and I were dismissed from the People of Praise. We were alone and without an income, but we were also free.

Since 1989, many members or former members of the People of Praise and the Sword of the Spirit covenant communities have approached Marie and me. These people have wanted support, advice and an understanding of what had happened to them. Having started out with such zeal and high hopes for serving the Lord, how could they have fallen into discouragement, such constant sense of failure and into a genuine loss of freedom? This book attempts to answer these questions. What happened to us and so many others was not an accident. It results from the very structure and principles underlying these groups.

Much of what we will see in the following pages applies specifically to these charismatic covenant communities. However, most of the analysis can also be applied to other kinds of renewal groups. What happened to us is not an isolated error but a fundamental misunderstanding of salvation, community, the Church, and God's will. This misunderstanding can and does occur in other movements, organizations, nondenominational churches and Catholic religious orders. Our hope is that this volume will shed light on the very real problem of the Christian's loss of freedom to false prophets.

While I bear full responsibility for the contents of this book, it would not have been possible without my wife, Marie. She supported me throughout our life in the community; I was a "true believer," while she remained somewhat skeptical. She has shared her insights, and we have discussed at great length everything in this book. Indeed, Marie has contributed substantively to many sections throughout this work. Without her help, this book would be shorter, less well-thought-out, and definitely less interesting.

My daughter Teresa helped type the original manuscript and offered some insights from her perspective as a child in the community. Tom Yoder of Ann Arbor, Michigan, and Bill Beatty generously made available rare unpublished materials. Fran Maier, formerly of the National Catholic Register, generously offered to read the text and gave some very useful suggestions. There are, of course, many others whom I could thank—men and women from several covenant communities who have shared their experiences with me and who have supported this project. This work is dedicated to our four children, Joseph Reimers, Teresa Stringham, Peter Reimers, and George Reimers, who lived and at times suffered from their parents' choice of a life that was at best "weird" and sometimes incomprehensible.

Most of the unpublished materials cited in this work and listed in the bibliography are stored and accessible in the University Archives of the University of Notre Dame.

CHAPTER 1.
THE BEGINNINGS

"News too good to be true!" "A new chance for the Catholic Church." "A new Pentecost!" With phrases like these, the students, teachers, theologians and others described the outbreak of the charismatic renewal in the late 1960's. In the wake of the Second Vatican Council a kind of craziness had taken hold within the Church. "Guitar (or folk) Masses" brought "The 59th Street Bridge Song" ("Feelin' Groovy") into the liturgy. Liturgical experimentation resulted in home masses where bread and wine were replaced with pizza and beer. Theologians made headlines by proclaiming "God is dead." Belief in things like the bodily resurrection of Christ, the reality of miracles, the authenticity of Scripture as God's word and the efficacy of prayer were widely dismissed as "irrelevant." In the name of the Council, everything that the Church once stood so solidly for was called into question, with theologians in the Catholic colleges and universities apparently leading the way.

When a small group of students at Duquesne University, and then a larger group at Notre Dame, experienced a profound movement of grace in answer to their prayers, a faith that seemed on the verge of extinction in the larger Church was being rediscovered. At first the students, then lay people all across the country flocked to charismatic prayer meetings to pray and praise God fervently, to experience the spiritual gifts of tongues, prophecy and healing, and to find a new life of faith. Almost overnight, the Pentecostal or charismatic movement emerged in the Catholic Church.

The characteristic form of this movement was the local prayer group. As few as a half dozen and as many as 2,000 Catholic Pentecostals would gather in a living room or parish hall or school room for loosely structured prayer and praise. Eventually, however, this loose association proved insufficient for many. Charismatics asked themselves what might be the next step. How can we move on in the Lord?

In the years of the Council and immediately after there was much talk of the importance of community in the life of the People of God. It was only natural for many charismatics to want to form charismatic communities. In 1969, The Word of God covenant community was established in Ann Arbor, Michigan, and in 1971, True House and the People of Praise were founded in South Bend, Indiana. These quickly became the normative form for charismatic renewal. The movement's leadership was largely drawn from these. The covenant community quickly became the ideal to which every group should aspire.

"The emergence of covenant communities is a development of major importance (within the charismatic renewal). By providing leadership resources, formation programs, growth seminars, and sharing across a large spectrum of human and spiritual needs, they have become a significant sign of the kingdom of God present in power."[5] So wrote the National Conference of Catholic Bishops in 1989. Subsequently a critique of these covenant communities has been growing. This critique centered largely on the contention that these groups are "shepherding-discipleship groups" that practice thought control—in more popular language, cults. Much of this critique has amounted to a series of allegations of exploitation, abuse of authority, arranged marriages, and deception of Church authorities. These critiques have indeed drawn much needed attention to these groups and their practices.[6] In several places the local Ordinaries have launched investigations in response to complaints by members and former members.

This book takes a close look at the lives of these groups. Its purpose is to analyze the foundational documents of the two main systems of covenant communities—The Sword of the Spirit[7] and the People of Praise (headquartered in South Bend, Indiana)—and to examine the life that is based on these documents. We will also look at significant articles and teachings by their founders and principal leaders. While doing this, it will be helpful to compare these writings with the Church's understanding of Christ's intentions for His people. We will see that these groups have not been reliable guides to Christian living for their Catholic members, that their structures and theological presuppositions militate against Catholics' life of faith and undermine their personal freedom.

The importance of the People of Praise and the Sword of the Spirit for the covenant community movement can hardly be overstated. The leaders and founders of these groups—Stephen B. Clark and Ralph Martin (The Word of God/Sword of the Spirit), Paul C. DeCelles and Kevin Ranaghan (People of Praise)—formulated the vision, developed the teachings, promulgated the principles and established the actual models that have inspired almost every other covenant community in North America.[8]

The Word of God community was founded in Ann Arbor, Michigan by Martin, Clark and several other young people associated with the charismatic prayer group in that college town. The organization grew quickly in numbers and influence. Easily one of the most dynamic and popular speakers in the early days of the Catholic charismatic movement, Martin became a key leader of the movement. His gift for powerful, moving prophetic utterances and speeches magnified his reputation as a man of God anointed to bring something new to the Church. The studious, understated Clark brought to the movement a note of sobriety and clear-headedness which won it respect from those concerned about emotional excess. Within three years of its founding, The Word of God was publishing *New Covenant*, which served as the movement's semi-official national publication until 2002. In the early 1970s, people—especially young people—were flocking from around the nation to join this new work of God.

By 1974 Cardinal Leon Suenens of Malines, Belgium had visited the Ann Arbor community and had begun to take a personal concern for the charismatic movement. When Charismatic leaders sought to bring the movement's annual conference to Rome for the Holy Year in 1975, Cardinal Suenens cleared the way and even arranged for Pope Paul VI to address the 8,000 participants. Eventually, in 1977, he came to invite that community and the People of Praise to establish a covenant community in Brussels, near the International Charismatic Renewal Office.

The beginnings of the People of Praise were similar, if less dramatic. In the summer and fall of 1971, two covenant communities emerged from the same charismatic prayer meeting. Jim Byrne, a senior at Notre Dame, gathered a community of students and recent graduates to form "True House." A few months later DeCelles and Ranaghan gathered a community consisting mainly of townspeople from South Bend. Within three years True House had collapsed from leadership problems. The People of Praise, however, grew in both size and influence. While the group in Ann Arbor published, the People of Praise distributed books and organized huge congresses that attracted up to 26,000 participants to the Notre Dame campus. To see Knute Rockne's stadium half-full of charismatics chanting "He's number one!"—referring to Jesus—was enough to convince almost anyone that something remarkable was happening. These events propelled Kevin Ranaghan into a position as spokesman and most visible theologian of the new movement. They also began to enrich the People of Praise financially.

At the closing Mass of the 1975 International Conference in Rome, several prophecies were spoken from the high altar at

St. Peter's Basilica by Ralph Martin and other known prophets. The theme of these prophecies was a coming period of "hard times" for Christians and for the Church.

> Because I love you, I want to show you what I am doing in the world today. ... Days of darkness are coming on the world, days of tribulation ... Supports that are there for my people now will not be there ... A time of darkness is coming on the world, but a time of glory is coming for my church, a time of glory is coming for my people. I will pour out on you all the gifts of my Spirit. I will prepare you for spiritual combat; I will prepare you for a time of evangelism that the world has never seen. ...[9]

These prophecies confirmed the community leaders in the basic direction they had chosen—to found a network of firmly committed communities, modeled on the People of Praise and The Word of God, to be a bulwark for God's people. The new support for God's people was to be strong covenant community. In the years to follow, both *New Covenant* magazine and the national conferences stressed the need for "committed relationships," authority, and community. During the years immediately after the Rome conference, communities dominated the National Service Committee of the Catholic Charismatic Renewal. The Committee sought to foster the covenant community as the ideal and logical development of the charismatic renewal. Charismatic Renewal Services became the joint outreach of the People of Praise and The Word of God.

The underlying vision throughout this period was to form a network of communities, and as the 1970s drew to a close, Clark, Martin, DeCelles and Ranaghan had achieved a partial success at a provisional union. In 1976, communities from Minneapolis-St. Paul, East Lansing (Michigan), Augusta (Georgia), Phoenix (Arizona), Muncie (Indiana), Baltimore, and other cities gathered at Notre Dame under the leadership of the Ann Arbor and South Bend groups for a Conference of Communities. In August 1977 the leaders from these and others gathered in South Bend to build their unity. But by 1980, serious strains had started to develop. In 1981, citing problems of vision and disagreements about the role of their communities in relation to the world, Paul DeCelles and Kevin Ranaghan announced to the "Association of Communities" that they would no longer work toward the planned unity with The Word of God. In the years to follow, the People of Praise fostered their own network of communities, which eventually became a system of branches of the People of Praise. The Word of God formed its communities into a network of communities called the Sword of the Spirit. Some time later, a third network was formed, the International Brotherhood of Covenant Communities. In 1990 the I.B.O.C.C. was granted canonical recognition by the Pontifical Council of the Laity.

From their earliest days covenant communities had been the object of concern on the part of some observers, and through the years reports surfaced alleging denominational indifferentism, abuse of authority and constraint of conscience, subjugation of women and cult-like tendencies. For the most part, others countered these concerns. Often theologically well qualified, these defenders saw great hope for the Church in these groups, or dismissed the concerns as the idle complaints of "disgruntled former members." However, two events brought the difficulties with some covenant communities to the fore. First was Bishop Albert Ottenweller's 1990 pastoral investigation of the Christ the King Covenant Community (a community of Sword of the Spirit) in Steubenville, Ohio. Second was the break between The Word of God and the Sword of the Spirit—and consequently between Clark and Martin). Bishop Ottenweller's investigation established clearly that in that community the abuses were real. Shortly thereafter, Ralph Martin acknowledged the seriousness of the abuses in the Sword of the Spirit.

It is this author's contention that these abuses are structural, arising precisely from a deeply flawed conception of what Christian community is. These communities are faulty at their very root. The ideas that underlie these groups have influenced the formation of almost every covenant community in North America. A close look at these foundations, then, will prove valuable not only for a critique of the Sword of the Spirit and the People of Praise, but also for the proper evaluation, understanding and guidance of other covenant communities, including those enjoying episcopal oversight and canonical recognition.

In 1978 Rev. Kilian McDonnell, who saw in covenant communities a positive hope for renewal and ecumenical progress, warned that without a proper ecclesiological understanding of their nature, such groups "will develop into another stream of Christianity, neither Orthodox, Protestant, Catholic, Anglican nor classical Pentecostal, but a vague enthusiastic mélange of churchless Christianity."[10] In fact, this development is well underway in both the Sword of the Spirit and the People of Praise. If other covenant communities are to bear fruit and if any covenant community is to be evaluated properly, a solid understanding of their ecclesiological role and of the lay person's vocation is vital. This book attempts to contribute to such an evaluation.

CHAPTER 2.
SOME KEY TERMS

"No one has ever lived in the circumstances we are living in. We can't learn from the past."[11] This principle, expressed at the very beginning of the Sword of the Spirit's "Training Course," underlay much of the thinking in the first decade and a half of covenant community life. The times and the situation were so different that all previous bets were off. The world was dramatically and decisively different from any other historical era. Furthermore, what God was doing was completely new and different. With the proper wisdom, one could draw limited guidance from the history of the Church, but such guidance was only provisional. A new wisdom was being offered.

In this new situation, many significant old terms were used, especially as the communities set up their leadership and pastoral systems. Old words acquired new meanings, often significantly different from the Church's original understanding. The result has been a certain clouding or masking of what these communities are about. The terms and their usage may be traditional enough, but the meaning is new. It is important then to clarify some key terms at the outset.

The first step is to examine some key ideas, with particular attention to how the Church understands them. These ideas are: Body of Christ, covenant, community and communion, pastor, charism and ecclesial community.

A. BODY OF CHRIST

From the movement's earliest days, the idea of the Body of Christ has had a new significance for Catholic charismatics. Chapters 12 through 14 of 1 Corinthians became primary texts for the new movement. In these chapters St. Paul presents the charismata precisely in the context of the properly functioning Body of Christ. The solutions to the inevitable problems concerning the function and ordering of the gifts were to be found by reflecting on the good and the harmony of the body. The operation of the spiritual gifts, together with the strong emotional impact of dynamic prayer meetings, gave a powerful experiential aspect to the notion of the Body of Christ. Indeed, we assumed—uncritically, for the most part—that what we were seeing was the Body of Christ as the early Church had experienced it. At early conferences speakers taught that while we used to speak of "the mystical Body of Christ," we now speak of "the Body of Christ." Such experiences, together with a flawed interpretation of the Lord's promise, "Where two or more are gathered in my name, there am I in the midst of them," (Mt. 18: 20) led to a error concerning the Body of Christ.

The truth is that the Church has never regarded a simple gathering of Christians as such—no matter how well-intentioned, committed, or devout they may be—as sufficient to constitute them as the Body of Christ. Rather only that is the Body of Christ which is organically joined to Christ in such a way that he is present in it as priest, prophet and king. That is to say, the Body of Christ is there only when the body is able to offer Jesus Christ's self-same sacrifice to the Father in an act of perfect worship (Priest), when it can proclaim authoritatively His saving word as He wants it to be understood (Prophet), and when it visibly manifests Christ's rule as Head over His flock and over all men (King). Thus the Body of Christ necessarily depends on Christ Himself for its existence and not on those who happen to be members.[12] In other words, not every Christian body—be it the Society of Jesus, the St. Ann's Altar-Rosary Society, or the People of Praise—is the Body of Christ. Only the Church, the local Church (or diocese) as well as the universal Church, is the Body of Christ.

On this subject, the distinctions found in Pope Pius XII's encyclical, *Mystici Corporis*, are especially helpful. Pius XII does not oppose mystical body of Christ to real body of Christ, in the charismatic sense mentioned above, but to the physical body of Christ (i.e., that human organism which Mary bore, which walked the Holy Land and which the nails pierced). Both the mystical and the physical body of Christ are the real body of Christ, but they exist in different modes. The Pope goes on to explain that the mystical body, so understood, is very different from a moral body, which is a group of people united for a common good or aim.[13] In this Pope's understanding, covenant communities count as moral bodies of Christians, but not as the Body of Christ.

Nevertheless, to this day, these covenant communities routinely refer to themselves as "the body" or the "body of Christ." As we shall see, this expression has serious consequences for the lives of their members.

B. COMMUNITY AND COMMUNION

The idea of "community" closely parallels that of "body," and "Christian community"—properly speaking—refers to the same reality as "Body of Christ." The difference between the two terms has to do with focus and connotation. In the expression "Body of Christ," structural elements and function come to the fore. "Community," on the other hand, points to the relationships within the group, by which the members share a bond of unity or communion.

In common usage, the "community" tends to be vaguer than "Body of Christ" since we tend to call any group of Christians united around a Christian value a Christian

Community." Thus the Franciscans and the parish St. Vincent de Paul Society might refer to themselves as Christian communities (although the Franciscans would more likely call themselves a "religious community"). In the full and proper sense, the Christian Community is the Body of Christ. To see this, we must consider the related notions of communion, fellowship and brotherhood.

The Christian community is the fellowship characterized by union with Christ and in Christ. This is described at Acts 2: 42-47. The prototypical Christian community at Jerusalem was marked by apostolic teaching of God's Word, the breaking of the bread (Eucharist), joyful coming together of the members and sharing of material goods. Pope St. John Paul II writes:

> Every community, if it is to be Christian, must be founded on Christ and live in him, as it listens to the word of God, focuses its prayer on the Eucharist, lives in a communion marked by oneness of heart and soul, and shares according to the needs of its members. (cf. Acts 2:42-47)[14]

Thus the community centers around Christ in the Word and Sacrament while it transforms human relationships and the management of earthly wealth.

We should take particular notice of the role of the Eucharist. Because of the real presence of Christ in the Eucharist, the gathering of the community around him is real; the suffering and risen Christ is present in their midst. By receiving holy Communion, the members of the community share an intimate communion with the Lord, a communion that draws the assembly into a true brotherhood in Christ. Cardinal Joseph Ratzinger, who eventually became Pope Benedict XVI, wrote, "The common visible sharing in the goods of Salvation (the holy things), especially in the Eucharist, is the source of the invisible communion among the sharers (the saints)."[15] Thus the Christian Community is most perfectly Christian communion when it celebrates the Eucharist and partakes of Communion. It is for this reason that Pope John Paul II could write, "The Church lives by the Eucharist."[16]

Holy Communion brings about communion among those who partake of it in faith and charity. This communion of the faithful is a kind of friendship arising from a shared love for Christ and from the shared awareness that they are all joined to him. This is an ontological reality, but it is also something to be experienced. Christians, especially as they gather around the altar, are to be united in heart and mind. This experience is fostered by the symbolism of the Liturgy and especially by the use of music. However, other experiences—such as retreats, conferences, days of renewal—can work powerfully to bring this unity of Christian love to conscious awareness. The truth is that for most Catholics their most powerful experiences of God's love and Christ's presence occur in communion with others, in shared experiences that both depend on and build up their communion with Christ. This experience of communion, of a shared love for Jesus and of being loved by him, powerfully draws human hearts to one another.

Christ said before His death, "If I be lifted up, I will draw all men to myself." That act of self-giving by which he draws all men is represented on the altar of the Eucharist, so that Christ is present to save, redeem and draw men and women to himself and form them into a community to worship the Father.[17]

> For by Christ's will there is in this sacrament a continual renewing of the mystery of the sacrifice of himself that Christ offered to the Father on the altar of the cross, a sacrifice that the Father accepted ...[18]

This is why the Eucharist is not only a sign, but also a cause of our unity.[19] But where the cause is lacking, so too is the effect. Therefore, to the extent that a group of Christians lacks the fullness of the Eucharist, its internal unity is wounded and defective, and it falls short of being an authentic Christian community.[20] This is why the Second Vatican Council could write, "No Christian community is built up which does not grow from and hinge upon the celebration of the Holy Eucharist."[21]

If we turn to the lived-experience of charismatic communal prayer, these theological truths about community and liturgy seemed pale before the warm and joyful experiences of the prayer meeting where regular members know each other, calling each other "brother" and "sister and hugging each other when they meet. As one friend put it, "*ex opere operato* just doesn't cut it for me any more" This Latin phrase, "from the work done", refers to the objective efficacy of the sacramental action. Thus when the priest in the confessional blesses the penitent and says the words of absolution, the penitent is forgiven, no matter how he feels or what the priest thinks. At the Mass, the entire congregation is united in the presence of the suffering and risen Christ, even if most in the congregation are distracted by crying babies and hapless fumbling by one of the altar servers. We recognize in faith that we are one in Christ, but as we sing and pray together in tongues at the prayer meeting, we *feel* our unity.

C. COVENANT

Covenant communities understand "covenant" to be "a solemn agreement that establishes a relationship." This concept is deliberately taken from the Scriptures, where covenants between human beings and—especially—covenants between God and human beings define much of human relationships. In the Bible there is the further characteristic that the covenant entails a curse on the one who violates it.[22] Covenant is understood to provide the basis for these communities.

Unlike a modern contract, a covenant establishes a personal relationship between the parties. Thus, while a contract stands or falls by the precise interpretation of its language (and this interpretation can be provided by a disinterested third party, like a judge), a covenant stands on the personal commitment of the parties to be loyal to each other and to its terms. The failure of a covenant is a moral failure. To break it is personally to injure your brother. The covenant-maker lays his character on the line. This is why the Lord characteristically charges Israel with moral fault in the Old Testament. Their failure to keep the covenant is not merely the violation of an agreement. It is infidelity, comparable to adultery. Because of this personal characteristic of covenants, to make a covenant entails a certain renunciation of freedom. Brothers and sisters in a covenant owe their lives in a certain way to each other. They are accountable, perhaps not legally, but morally. They stand by each other "no matter what."

Concerning our lives as Christians, two things are worth noting about covenants: 1) Christ established the definitive covenant between God and man, and 2) Christians do not ordinarily refer to themselves as a "covenant people" as Israel did. To go in detail into these two points would, of course, be itself a major project far beyond our scope here, but a few points do need to be made about them.

The covenant established by God in Christ on Calvary is definitive not simply because God has promised no further covenant. Rather, a further covenant is neither possible nor conceivable. On Calvary God gave us all that He has to offer. He gave all His love. For atonement he offered His own Son as the sacrifice of reparation; beyond this act there is no further remedy for sin. For our new life, Christ poured out his Holy Spirit from the cross so that we might live by the very life he has lived. For our redeemed lives we have not simply a new law but a new Spirit, we become new creations. In the Eucharist, which is the same sacrifice as the Cross, each Christian is fully joined to Christ.

For our common life the crucified Christ draws us all to himself on the cross and allows us to enter as a worshipping assembly into his perfect act of worship before the Father. There can be no more perfect worship than this, because we have nothing more perfect to offer God than what Christ has offered. The very fact that it is God himself, then, who offers himself as the covenant means that there can be no further covenant. Pope John Paul II taught,

> The Church is the new community of individuals, instituted by Christ as a "calling together" of all those called to be a part of the new Israel in order to live the divine life, according to the graces and demands of the covenant established by the sacrifice of the cross.[23]

Paradoxically, this reality explains why Christians do not normally refer to themselves as a covenant people, as the people of Israel has.[24] For if Jesus Christ Himself is the new covenant, then our focus is on Him and not on the covenant aspect. Indeed, Christ has chosen to realize His covenant among us by becoming present to us sacramentally. So, by baptism we are not just joined spiritually to Christ, but we enter into His own death and resurrection. Although Our Lord atoned for all our sin by His redemptive death, when He said, "Father, forgive them," Jesus applies that atonement personally to each of us as we bring our sins to Him in the Sacrament of Reconciliation. And as Christ saved us and poured out His Spirit on us from the cross, the crucified and risen Lord saves us and pours out His Spirit on us through that self-same sacrifice offered sacramentally at the Mass. Indeed, it is precisely at the Eucharistic assembly that the blood of the covenant is poured out and shared, so that this assembly is the people of the New Covenant. Yet because Christ Himself, sacramentally present, is this new covenant, we usually speak of this people in terms of their communion with Him—the "fellowship of believers" —and as the Eucharistic assembly—the Church.[25]

Precisely here we find two central elements that build

up the Church and form our consciousness of Church: communion and covenant. Both are rooted in the Eucharist, and both address a deep need of the human heart. The experience of communion is the consciousness of belonging, of being important to others and—even more significant—being part of something transcendentally important. The communion of saints is not just a doctrine, but it is also experienced as the sharing of a common life and love with the martyrs of the Roman persecutions, the 12th-century Franciscans and the 16th-century Carmelites, with the apostles and holy women throughout Church history and with Christians around the world. It has a direct contemporary significance as well, for in this communion one feels himself as joined with other brothers and sisters who share the same values, goals and loves. The Christians being persecuted today in Nigeria and China are our brothers and sisters. And in this consciousness of communion one experiences acceptance and love and a sense of common mission in Christ.

The element of covenant gives a kind of juridical or legal structure to this communion. The covenant defines the relationship within which the communion is experienced. As such, it adds to communion the notion of obligation. Under a covenant one responds to the love received in communion on the basis of commitment and responsibility, and not simply out of gratitude. The covenant-partner owes a certain response to the others in the covenant. Because he is (in a way) juridically committed to the communion, he has yielded certain freedoms he had previously enjoyed. He "owes" it to his covenant brothers and sisters to keep up his part. To violate it is a kind of disloyalty. Indeed, this is why it is so serious a matter for one, having received salvation, to repudiate it; salvation is based on a covenant in Christ. As a commitment that carries a moral orientation, the covenant imposes a certain objective continuity, which endures even when the warm and consoling sense of communion may be absent. As such, covenant constitutes a powerful complement to communion.

From these considerations it is easy to see that the idea of covenant community can be powerfully attractive. Participants in the charismatic renewal movement have typically enjoyed strong consolations from the Lord. At charismatic Masses, prayer meetings and large rallies they very often find themselves caught up in an almost tangible sense of communion, and from this arises a strong thirst for unity. Standing in a large arena full of fellow Christians singing and praising God in unison, one can easily imagine that Christ himself is there embracing all and ready to welcome them into his Kingdom. This was indeed my own experience at my first charismatic conference at Notre Dame in 1972, as the entire basketball arena of the Joyce Center erupted in joyful praise of God. The impulse is precisely to find a way to institutionalize this communion without killing it. The notion of covenant provides this institutional (or better, constitutional) key. Where most institutional forms tend to be bureaucratic and impersonal, the covenant is a living, personal reality. It is a commitment to fidelity in love, very much like a family relationship. And indeed, covenant communities regularly use "family" metaphors, calling each other "brother" and "sister" and comparing their covenant with the marriage relationship.[26]

D. PASTOR AND PASTORAL CARE

Jesus Christ is the "Good Shepherd," the "One Shepherd" of the one flock. All others who came before him were "robbers and thieves." Unlike the hired hand, who is not a shepherd, the one true good shepherd lays down his life for his sheep. The hired hand runs away to save his own skin. (Jn 10:1-13) Now these famous texts do more than to provide us with the characteristics of a good shepherd. They identify the Good Shepherd, Christ himself. There is but one Pastor of the Christian people; He is the Lord Jesus.

This being the case, we need to account for those in the

Church who are called "pastors" and whom the Scriptures too call pastor or shepherd. (We may note in passing that precisely the same questions arise in connection with Matt. 23: 9, where Our Lord forbids us to call our spiritual leaders by the name "Father.") What Jesus says about the One Good Shepherd makes sense to us only if 1) either no man serves as pastor, and in some mystical way Jesus pastors every soul, or 2) the human pastor is so related or ordered to Christ that his actions are those of Christ.

In the Church's understanding, this second option is the case. The priest or pastor, acting as such, acts *in persona Christi*. What he does as minister of the Word of God and of the Sacraments is the action of Christ. Thus, while a good pastor ought to lay down his life for his parish or diocese, whenever that pastor celebrates the Eucharist, the Good Shepherd is there laying down His life for the flock, calling them by name and feeding them.[27] And by His preaching, administering the Sacrament of Baptism and hearing confessions, the pastor is there warding off the Enemy who would snatch the sheep and scatter them. Presiding over the flock in the name and person of the Good Shepherd who has laid down His life in obedience to the Father, the pastor leads his flock to the worship that will one day be eternally theirs to give in heaven.[28]

This means that only they are pastors who have been designated by the Church and ordained in Christ to exercise sacramentally the ministry of the one Good Shepherd. In recent years we have used the word "pastor" somewhat loosely (as well as the word "ministry") to refer to any kind of Christian counseling and spiritual caregiving. Thus, in hospitals we see religious and lay persons serving as "pastoral assistants or counselors." In his exhortation on the laity John Paul II wrote,

> However, **the exercise of such tasks does not make pastors of the lay faithful**. In fact, a person is not a minister simply in performing a task, but through sacramental ordination. Only the Sacrament of Orders gives

> the ordained ministry a particular participation in the office of Christ, the Shepherd and Head.[29]

Properly speaking, only a priest can be a pastor. The importance of this is that members of covenant communities regularly regard their leaders as pastors, as well as those appointed by these leaders to exercise pastoral authority.

E. CHARISM AND RELIGIOUS COMMUNITIES

If only the local Church is the Christian community (as noted above), nevertheless, the Catholic Church is filled with "communities" and communal structures. Religious sisters, brothers and priests live in communities. Lay persons may form and enter lay associations that—by any reasonable definition of the term—amount to communities. And these communities are Christian. Indeed, the *Code of Canon Law* states:

> Christ's faithful may freely establish and direct associations to serve charitable or pious purposes or which foster the Christian vocation in the world, and they may hold meetings to pursue these purposes by common effort. [30]

There is therefore no *a priori* reason why Catholic charismatics might not gather into communal groups marked by a high degree of mutual commitment, sharing and sacrifice. There is no reason why they may not call such groups "covenant communities." Indeed, the Church has expressly authorized a fellowship of such communities.

In fact, the Church expressly grants great freedom to the faithful in pursuing apostolic initiatives. In the Second Vatican Council's Decree on the Apostolate of Lay Persons we read:

> The Holy Spirit sanctifies the People of God through the ministry and the sacraments. However for the exercise of

> the apostolate he gives the faithful special gifts besides (cf. 1 Cor. 12:7) ... From the reception of these charisms, even the most ordinary ones, there arises for each of the faithful the right and duty of exercising them in the Church and in the world for the good of men and the development of the Church, of exercising them in the freedom of the Holy Spirit who "breathes where he will" (Jn. 3:8), and at the same time in communion with his brothers in Christ, and with his pastors especially.[31]

Vatican II was indeed a council for the laity, emphasizing the Church as the People of God and not only as a hierarchically ordered society. *Lumen gentium* stresses that the call to holiness is universal. Both *Gaudium et spes* and *Apostolicam actuositatem* (The Decree on the Apostolate of Lay People) propose that lay people can become involved in or even initiate a rich variety of apostolates. However, never does the Church—neither in the Council nor in any other authoritative source—allow that simply anything a lay group proposes to do in the name of Christ or his Church is an acceptable exercise of this freedom. The text cited above indicates the parameters governing this freedom.

First of all, the Council states, "The Holy Spirit sanctifies the People of God through the ministry and the sacraments." The work of sanctifying, that is, of bringing the love of God to life within us and of making us holy, is accomplished through the ministry and the sacraments. "Ministry" here means the ordained priesthood and not a lay service or charismatic apostolate. Whatever else the lay faithful may do to serve their fellow human beings, they cannot make them holy.[32] Therefore, a lay association cannot have its function the sanctification of its members.

This relates closely to the point we emphasized above, that only the local Church (the diocese) is the Christian community, properly speaking, for only this community is the community of salvation. This is the community which Christ has gathered as his holy People, saved by baptism into his death and joined to himself by the Eucharist. Cardinal Ratzinger writes,

> In fact, the community, in receiving the Eucharistic presence of the Lord, receives the entire gift of salvation, and shows ... that it is the image and presence of the one, holy, catholic and apostolic Church.[33]

This community is therefore the fundamental and underlying reality for every group of Christians. Whatever associations or community they may build are constructed on this foundation of the brotherhood they share in Christ through the ministry of ordained priests, especially in the sacraments. Cardinal Ratzinger (Benedict XVI) notes, "The individual organization is justified only insofar as it serves the brotherhood of the whole community (i.e., the parish)."[34] Thus, the text from the *Decree on the Apostolate of the Laity* specifies that the charisms (including the charisms that lead to the forming of a new group or ecclesial community) be exercised "in communion with his brothers in Christ, and with his pastors especially."

These comments so far have been limiting and negative, defining what a lay organization or ecclesial community is not. More important, of course, is to speak to what is permitted and even encouraged. Precisely in this context the Second Vatican Council speaks of charisms, gifts of the Holy Spirit. "However for the exercise of the apostolate he gives the faithful special gifts besides (cf. 1 Cor. 12:7)." These gifts or charisms have been given for Christians to perform apostolic works. These charisms may be extraordinary, but they need not be.[35]

The effect of a charism may well go beyond the simple equipping of someone for service in the Church. The charism may well constitute the basis for a communal grouping within the Church. This is especially true of what are called the charisms of founders of religious orders. The effect of such a charism is twofold[36]: First, it presents a new way of following Christ, a new model for the practical living of the Christian life. As such, it constitutes the basis for a form of communal life. For example, Mother Teresa's vision or charism for loving Christ in the poorest of the poor, one at a time, is the key to the life of the Missionaries of Charity, which she gathered around her. The second effect of the charism is that it is prophetic and makes the one who embodies it into a prophet, very similar to the prophets of Scripture. The charismatic addresses the "signs of the times" with a divine interpretation. Mother Teresa's charism directly addresses and challenges the gross materialism and degradation of the person that is so characteristic of this era. Thus the charismatic founder fills the role both of spiritual father (or mother) to those who find a new spiritual life through him and of the prophet to the rest of the Church and the world.

The clearest examples of such charismatic community can be found in the founding of various religious orders, but the same principles may well apply in the formation of lay groups and associations. Within the charismatic renewal movement, we have seen the prayer groups in El Paso, Texas, called to a selfless witness of help to the poor who scavenge their living in the dumps of Ciudad Juarez, Mexico. The Emmanuel Community in Paris, France has undertaken a vibrant ministry of street evangelization to win disillusioned young people for Christ. Lay preachers like Ralph Martin have effectively called many Catholics back to a deep reverence for God's holiness and to love of his word. These charisms can form and have often formed the basis for groups with their own apostolates.

It is vital to recognize, of course, that the charism is not the basis for the fundamental unity in Christ among the members. The basis of that unity can only be Christ's own act of redemption, communicated through the sacrament of Baptism. It is, however, the foundation of an experience of that unity and for a common apostolate and mission. Therefore, the charismatic community must always be regarded as a part of the Christian community, and not as being the Christian community itself. Its leaders might relate as spiritual father or mother to their followers and be called "Reverend Mother" or "Father Abbot." But these never take the place of the apostles Christ has entrusted with governance of his people.

So it is true that the leader of a charismatic or religious community may well enjoy a certain authority in the lives of the members of the group. As the preceding discussion of "pastor" has made clear, this is not a fundamental pastoral or teaching authority for their Christian lives as a whole. This leader is not competent (as a community leader) to form the body of Christ or to pastor the individuals in it. However, since the basic charism of the group by its very nature defines a particular kind of response to the call of the Gospel, since it proposes a particular way of following Christ, then the leader can authoritatively teach that charism and guide the members into that pattern of life. So, for example, while the study of the Old Testament in the original languages is a very good thing for a Christian to do, Mother Teresa would probably deny permission to one of her sisters to undertake graduate studies in theology. One who felt strongly called to such a life of study is doubtless not called to the life of the Missionaries of Charity. The founder or leader has the authority to preserve the group according to its distinctive charism and to help individuals discern their role in it (or outside it) according to that charism.

It goes without saying that such a leader has no authority or right to presume to judge concerning the fundamental Christian commitment of one who is not called to live that charism. Nor can such a leader rightfully claim that the pattern of life for his or her group is definitive for the Christian life of all.

In his Apostolic Exhortation, *Christifideles laici*, Pope John Paul II has given five "criteria of ecclesiality" that must be met by lay groups (*Christifideles laici*, 30). They are:

1. *the primacy of the call to holiness;*
2. *the responsibility of professing the Catholic faith. "For this reason every association of the lay faithful must be a forum where*

the faith is proclaimed as well as taught ***in its total content.****" (emphasis added):*

3. *the witness to a strong and authentic communion in filial relationship to the Pope and local bishops;*
4. *conformity to and participation in the Church's apostolic goals, and*
5. *a commitment to a presence in human society.*

The point of these criteria is precisely that the ecclesial community or association must live and work as a part of the whole Church, even if it is not necessarily formally recognized by the Church. Properly related to the Church, such groups can have immense power for the apostolate. Often inspired by the Holy Spirit and reflecting the social nature of the human person, these groups can answer a deep yearning for the Christians who want to give themselves more fully to the service of the Lord. They provide a way for the Church effectively to minister to those in need, according to the authentic signs of the times.

Highly committed charismatic communities, directing their efforts towards evangelism, service to the poor, ecumenical friendship, the fostering of charismatic prayer, etc. have an important place in the life of the Church. We must examine whether the way chosen by the Sword of the Spirit and the People of Praise was the proper one.

One of the most heartening things for me at my first prayer meetings was to find a group of people, including some with theological education, who believed that God answers prayers. As an undergraduate at Notre Dame in the mid-1960s, when everyone was a theologian—or tried to be—I learned that God does not listen to prayers, *not really*. Furthermore, because God is love and wants us to love, unchaste behavior on the weekends, was not really sinful as long as we felt love. It was refreshing to find this group at the prayer meeting who believed those things that Catholics had always believed until recently.

CHAPTER 3.

THE COMMON ROOT – *BUILDING CHRISTIAN COMMUNITIES*

Most of us who were involved at the time believed that the covenant communities sprang up as a direct response to the Holy Spirit's inspiration. We felt a call to share our lives and faith more fully, and thirty of us began to meet in a house just two blocks from the Notre Dame campus. As we prayed about forming community, the Lord himself seemed to ratify this desire. In the early days of covenant community, all of us—leaders and ordinary members—talked constantly about the need to "keep our eyes on the Lord" to follow only him. We thought that we were discerning together what our community should be. In fact, however, the vision for our communities had already been articulated well in advance of the first stirrings of the charismatic renewal. Stephen B. Clark's *Building Christian Communities* appeared in 1972. The ideas in this book provided the fundamental conception of community on which both the Sword of the Spirit and the People of Praise were based. Therefore, an understanding of the key ideas in this book is essential to understanding these groups.

In 1981 the People of Praise separated from the Word of God/Sword of the Spirit and disavowed its connection with Stephen B. Clark and his writings. In particular, People of Praise leaders have argued recently that criticisms of Clark's thought and approaches do not apply to their group because of this repudiation. Nevertheless, *Building Christian Communities* is foundational to that group as well as to the Sword of the Spirit for two reasons:

First, the main ideas for the book were formed in the context of Clark's work and discussions in the early and mid-1960's with a group whose members included Paul C. DeCelles and Kevin M. Ranaghan, the eventual founders of People of Praise. This work, *Building Christian Communities*, expresses much of this group's common vision. A set of minutes, dated September 2, 1964, has survived from those meetings at Notre Dame. Even before the beginning of the charismatic renewal, this group was outlining plans to form a community which would be the nucleus of the Christian renewal at Notre Dame.

> The main goal is to **create a church**, and it is important that this be not lost sight of. An essential part of being a leader should be to **have an ecclesiastical function** (to consciously help maintain the life and spirit of the church).[37] (Emphasis added)

The document is the detailed outline of proposed structures for a tightly knit Christian community which would take the leadership in forming Christian life at Notre Dame. The proposal is full of arcane terminology: The leader is called the "dictator" and his assistant the "et 2," the core of the community is the "null set," and new recruits are formed by "formers." What is especially important for our purpose here is the conception of the Church at work behind this document. The sacramental character of the Church hardly appears. The Church is

> the community of people who are holy in Christ. A community dedicated to God in and through Christ, whose internal and external relations are patterned on the model Christ gave us.[38]

In other words, the Church is seen in social terms and as constituted primarily by its members and their character. Thus it follows that ordained priests are to play a secondary role in this renewal project. This is because, according to Clark, priests have been poorly trained and are not generally capable of being Christian leaders. The document states, "Priests have a functional role within the Christian community; they are not a trained elite."[39] The ideas so artlessly presented in this memo would find their refinement in Clark's *Building Christian Communities.*

The second reason is that in the summer of 1971 Ranaghan and DeCelles taught a course on community to the Apostolic Institute's deacon training program in South Bend and invited interested persons from the weekly charismatic prayer meeting to attend. Those who attended these talks were invited that August to meet for the purpose of forming the community eventually named People of Praise. The course was based on the manuscript for Clark's book. To understand both groups, then, it is important to understand *Building Christian Communities.*

A. ENVIRONMENTS AND EMERGENT LEADERSHIP AS PASTORAL TOOLS

Building Christian Communities offers a pastoral strategy for the church in the post-Vatican II years. To some extent, this strategy is based on sound principles and insights. Of these the two central concepts are *environments* and *emergent leadership.*

Clark identifies the group *environment* as a bearer of group values and as a primary agent in fostering these values. Most Christians today live and work in social environments that do not support their Christian faith, but which quite often militate against it. An office may be a hotbed of greed and back-biting, and the dormitory one of lust. To mention the name of Jesus in any way but as a vulgarity may open one to ridicule and rejection. Clark's insight is that for most Christians such environments will weaken their commitment to Christ. Conversely, if Christians could spend most of their lives in explicitly Christian environments, their faith would grow stronger.

In light of this, it makes sense for pastoral leaders to try to find ways to foster the formation and growth of such environments and to stabilize them institutionally. In other words, Clark calls for the formation of fairly small communities within the church, communities which would be "primary groups" for their members. Each community should be large enough so that normal membership changes would not fundamentally alter the life of the group, but small enough so that everyone knows everyone else, even if only by sight. Such a group could be a powerful support for the growth in faith and apostolic effectiveness of its members.

The second element necessary for the formation of such communities is natural, "emergent leadership." Clark points out that besides appointed leadership (e.g., ordained and assigned to this parish), leadership by qualification (e.g., holds a Ph.D.), there is natural *emergent leadership*. That is, there are some people who, in virtue of an almost instinctive grasp of human nature combined with a dynamic personality, are able to get other people relating to one another in a way that fosters their sense of community and common purpose. They are "natural leaders" who can bring others together. To foster Christian community, then, a wise and necessary strategy is to identify such leaders and call on their strengths. Such persons are a valuable pastoral resource.

Without a doubt, Clark has rediscovered some important principles for forming community, principles which can be a genuine value for pastoral planning. However it is important also to note that these are purely natural principles. John Henry Newman refers warmly to the educational value of the student environment in the university. Students often are the best teachers for each other as they grapple with intellectual issues. And partially to account for a disappointing basketball season several years ago, Notre Dame coach Muffet McGraw explained that although her team had many talented players, no one of them emerged as a team leader. Every team needs that one or two players who can "spark" the rest to their best effort in the clutch. However, because faith is concerned essentially with a supernatural reality and is itself a theological virtue, such merely natural means cannot be the core of a pastoral plan. Christian environments led by natural leaders may help the life of faith, but they cannot directly affect it by making faith, hope, and love grow. Holiness comes from another source. Here we might recall St. John Vianney, the Curé of Ars, a priest with few compelling personal traits, who spent his pastoral life in deep prayer and hearing confessions. He powerfully transformed the spiritual life of his own village of Ars and the surrounding regions. The secret of his pastoral success was complete fidelity to the Faith and his personal holiness.

B. PROBLEMS WITH THE BOOK

Had Clark contented himself with an account of the factors mentioned above, *Building Christian Communities* would have stood as a potentially useful contribution. However, he plainly has more in mind than a modest contribution. *Building Christian Communities* portrays the pastoral structures of the Church as being in crisis and plainly warns that they are in danger of collapse. Thus the remedies that this book offers are not simply aids to help improve parish and diocesan life, but instead a plan to rescue the entire Church—a replacement for the moribund parish and diocesan structures. "There has to be a major structural change for Christianity to be able to survive in the modern world. The present parish system cannot do the job that needs to be done. It must be replaced by many basic Christian communities."[40] Though characteristically understated, Clark's viewpoint is apocalyptic. Clark's belief that he has found the key to the pastoral renewal and restructuring of the Church lead to several serious difficulties.

1. De-emphasis of the sacraments

Throughout the ensuing analysis of both Sword of the Spirit and People of Praise we will see this to be a serious problem. Nowhere in *Building Christian Communities* can one detect any trace at all of the doctrine that the Eucharist is the cause of our unity in Christ, that it is the "source and summit" of the life in Christ, that "the Church lives by the Eucharist." The book treats the sacraments (and liturgical life of the parish) as incidental to the main project of building community. Thus Clark speaks of the parish as a kind of service organization, providing its clientele with liturgies and sacraments.[41] He draws an implicit contrast between the typical priestly activity of planning liturgies and the work of pastoring. What this all really means is that Clark sharply de-emphasizes precisely that which Christ has given his Church to make it one. This provided a kind of intellectual shock for me personally. Thinking that I ought to know what the Second Vatican Council had to say about renewal of the Church—and the People of Praise was intended to help renew the Church—I read the Council documents. Reading that the Eucharist is the source and summit of the Christian life, I realized that this was not true of the life in our community. This was one of the first of my doubts about the People of Praise. This leads to the second difficulty.

2. The illegitimate distinction between pastor and priest

This is virtually a hallmark of Stephen Clark's thought. Indeed, his later work, *Unordained Elders and Renewal Communities*, explicitly attempts to provide historical support for the idea that one can be a pastor of the Christian community without having received Holy Orders. This idea is present and operative in *Building Christian Communities*, and it is particularly important.[42]

For Stephen Clark, the pastoral role is governmental, but not in the modern sense. The pastor is not involved in making, administering and judging according to impersonal laws that pertain to a given populace. Rather he is an *elder*, a senior man who oversees the lives and the common life of those entrusted to him so that they are formed individually and as a group according to the ideal of the community.[43] The ideal for such a pastor might well be the traditional village elder. He knows everyone and is personally concerned for them. In place of abstract law and impartial justice, he rules according to wisdom and love. He is the one who gives the community its form. Indeed without his eldership the community would soon cease to be. To interfere with his eldership is to change the character, the nature of the community and fundamentally to alter its integrity. Clark writes, "Not to respect the autonomy of a community in the choice of its leaders is to destroy the community or to absorb it into another."[44]

There is no essential reason why an elder/pastor, as conceived in this way, must also be an administrator of the sacraments and president of the assembly for worship.[45] If it is possible, it is best and most normal for the two to be combined. However, it is not essential. The principal benefit that accrues from having an elder ordained is that he is then "tied into" the larger Church. As the earlier discussion of the concept "pastor" makes clear, this distinction cannot be valid. The pastor of the Christian community is that precisely in virtue of his capacity as a minister of the sacraments. Only he can bring the whole Christ to the people.

Two serious difficulties flow from Clark's distinction between pastoring and sacramental administration. First, the life of faith is divorced from the life of grace. By "life of faith" here we mean the life that Christians lead. In Clark's conception, this is primarily the life of the Christian community. It is the life which is governed by the pastor-elder (or body of elders). This life is governed by tangible parameters: the community's pattern of life, its traditions, the teaching and direction and correction of the elders. However, grace is invisible. It is a reality which comes directly from God and has no natural origin. By the sacraments it may well come through visible realities, but it is not caused by the natural properties of those things.[46] As such, then, grace can operate independently of the social dynamics of the Christian community. The life of grace is the response to or—better—the conversation with God as he works directly and invisibly in the soul. If the life of faith is that which is governed by the unordained elder of the Christian community, then the response to grace must be primarily interior. Given the means at his disposal, it is very hard to see how the unordained pastor can foster—much less bring into being—this life of grace. Indeed, it is conceivable that the "life of faith" (i.e., the life in the Christian community as it pertains to this person) might conflict with the life of grace. Thus by grace the Holy Spirit may move in a way that demands an unusual response (thus St. Francis of Assisi), one which the elder does not discern and which may be counter to his understanding of that person's role in the community.

This had practical import for personal spirituality in community. Members were generally encouraged to spend time in prayer every day, and of course that was very good. Members were also to meet regularly (ideally every week) with their personal "head" or pastoral leader. Frequently, these meetings began with a question about the member's prayer life. More often that not, the head would ask, "So what is the Lord telling you in prayer?" This seems innocuous enough, but in fact it was manipulative. Having asked the question, the head (or pastoral leader) would have to comment on it, and that comment was seldom helpful and sometimes wrong. For instance, if it seemed that the Lord was actually communicating something (and for many of us, there were rare moments when it seemed that God might be speaking to us), the head would direct the member to a firmer commitment to the community and its endeavors.

Here we might remember St. Mother Teresa's "call within a call". While riding a train to Darjeeling and praying in her seat, Sister Teresa heard the Lord inviting her to serve him in the poorest of the poor. At this time, she had been serving Christ as a teacher in a Catholic school, which was not compatible with serving Christ in the gutters. (Teachers must prepare lesson plans, grade papers, and occasionally meet with parents.) God did speak to her, and after years of working with her own order's leaders and with Church authorities, her call within a call was confirmed. Sister Teresa did not need the discernment of an unordained, but emergent leader to tell her what God was *really* saying to her.

3. The downplaying of intellectual formation

Non-members of the People of Praise and Sword of the Spirit often remark on the high intellectual level of both groups. From their earliest days their membership has included a high percentage of college graduates, and their initial leaders held advanced degrees. Nevertheless there is a decisive anti-intellectual attitude in both groups, which is seen in *Building Christian Communities.*

For centuries the Church has insisted on the thorough intellectual formation of its clergy, particularly in theology and philosophy. Clark's emphasis on "emergent leadership" and his criticism of seminary preparation go hand-in-hand.[47] What is necessary, Clark states, is not that the leaders of the Christian people have theoretical knowledge of doctrinal fine points and historical polemics, but that they be able to lead others into Christian character, service, love of the brethren, and obedience to the Lord. The fundamental doctrines of the faith concerning the Trinity, Christ's redeeming death, the Resurrection of the dead and eternal life can be quickly and easily understood. The essential task is to translate these into life. For Clark, the primary focus of leadership formation should be on those skills and character traits that enable one to lead others deeper into Christ.

In fact, the leaders of the Sword of the Spirit (The Word of God) and the People of Praise eventually made a serious effort to implement such a training program with an eye to training pastors and priests for their communities. Together with a group of Protestant leaders, Stephen Clark, Ralph Martin, Paul DeCelles, and Kevin Ranaghan planned the founding of a Leadership Training Institute with the following goals:

> *a. to affect the spiritual and academic leadership of the Church;*
>
> b. to bring unity and compatibility between emerging communities;
>
> c. to train and equip teachers to provide protection for the Body of Christ
>
> d. to help deprogram ministers with only an academic mind-bent and increase their ability to discern spiritually when confronted by worldly expertise and wisdom.[48]

Less than one month before this proposal was adopted (It was never implemented.), Clark outlined his proposal on intellectual matters in a memo to community leaders.[49] This was intended to describe the intellectual basis of the Leadership Training Institute. Clark begins by noting that members of the communities need protection from worldly intellectual influences. "We need to break the tie of respect for the worldly academic environment and tradition and plant our people in a Christian one,"[50] he writes. There is an element of truth to his concern; certainly, the Christian cannot blindly accept the pronouncements of academic experts. To some extent, pride, ambition, confusion can all tend to corrupt the minds of even good Christian thinkers. But Clark's critique and solution are radical, going far beyond cautionary steps. The following are some principles Clark proposes for intellectual formation.

> We should not have "intellectuals." We should only have pastors and evangelists who are trained well to think and to teach.
>
> We should only give the right type of persons training in Christian thinking ... those who are psychologically healthy, **who have the ability to do Christian service well, who are committed, who are submissive, who can live well in brotherly relationships.** (emphasis added)
>
> Discipleship should be the mode of training. Those who are being trained should receive personal formation at the same time, both so that they are taught how to think as Christians and so that their personal difficulties are dealt with.

The next quote shows clearly that Clark's disapproval reaches far beyond Bultmann and Renan—indeed, so far as to reach Sts. Anslem, Bonaventure, and Thomas Aquinas.

> We should not present theology but teaching. "Theology" would be the kind of instruction given since the Middle Ages, which is structured on the model of secular academic disciplines. It orients people to approach Christian teaching with the same mental attitudes and approaches that they would use to secular disciplines. It is theoretical and speculative. "Teaching" would be the kind of teaching given during the patristic period and among many since then.[51]

The basis of Clark's approach is the rejection of learning and understanding truth in favor of applying truth practically in imitation of community leaders (i.e., discipleship).[52] Such a position may seem attractive in many ways, and the proposal that the pastoral candidate be given "handson" training has merit. However, the traditional intellectual formation of pastors is indispensable.[53] The reason for this is, in part, that the priest and ruler of God's people should have a thoroughgoing knowledge of the things of God.

There is also a further consideration, one especially crucial to recall when dealing with renewal groups and communities. In his PostSynodal Exhortation, *Pastores dabo vobis*, Pope John Paul II wrote:

> Only a sound philosophy can help candidates for the priesthood to develop a reflective awareness of the fundamental relationship that exists between the human spirit and truth, that truth which is revealed to us fully in Jesus Christ.[54]

Far from being an intellectual conceit or an ancillary exercise, intellectual study—especially of theology—is essential if faith is to be grounded in truth.

The covenant community approach to the intellectual life and theology stands in sharp contrast with that of Pope Saint John Paul II. He writes,

> Reason cannot eliminate the mystery of love which the cross represents, while the cross can give reason the answer which it seeks. [...] Of itself, philosophy is able to recognize the human being's ceaselessly self-transcendent orientation toward the truth; and, with the assistance of faith, it is capable of accepting the "foolishness" of the cross as the authentic critique of those who delude themselves that they possess the truth, when in fact they run aground on the shoals of a system of their own devising. [...] Here we see not only the border

> between reason and faith, but also the space where the two may meet.[55]

For John Paul II, the task of reason was not simply to determine how best to live or to share a community life. Indeed, I remember talking about Jesus with a brother in the People of Praise and being startled that this good brother (he was good and a friend) held to an Adoptionist view of the divinity of Christ. This is contrary to the teaching of the Council of Nicea, professed every Sunday in the Creed, that Jesus has both a human and a divine nature. Even if not well understood by most believers, it is a central truth of the faith. The task of reason is to attain to truth. Indeed, the very prologue to *Fides et Ratio* is a paean to the human project to discover truth that will give meaning to life. This is not only a truth for social or ecclesiastical leaders. It is a truth that every human person can possess and hold for his own. The pursuit and acquisition of truth is both a right and a duty for every human person.

Classically, theology is characterized as *fides quaerens intellectum*, faith seeking understanding. Although it uses natural human powers of reason and analysis, theology rests on principles or premises that transcend human experience, that is, on Revelation. What is important to stress is that revelation has an authentic truth content. There is one and only one God and in Him Three Persons (and not one or some other number). This statement of doctrine is true; the Catholic faith is that this corresponds to reality, and any statement inconsistent with this does not correspond to reality. From the relations among the truths divinely revealed and between them and naturally known truths, rational relations can be discovered and from them further truths known. These are the subject of theology.[56] I belabor this point because there has been throughout the modern era a marked tendency to relegate religion to the emotions or to moral behavior (which is what Clark's book does). The presumed importance of religious doctrines is supposed to be that they inspire certain good sentiments or support worthwhile life commitments and moral stances and not that they state the truth. The value of traditional seminary formation of priests, with its strong academic emphasis on theology and philosophy, is that it underscores the objectivity and rationality of the faith.

Clark's downplaying of intellectual formation is consistent with his conception of the nature of pastoring. In this context, what is important is that the pastors be able to lead others to a commitment and be able to hold faithfully to that commitment. However, two dangers come from this. The first is that of falling into doctrinal indifferentism, by which the doctrinal disagreements among Christians are relegated to unimportance or irrelevance (as was the case with my friend). Indeed, as we shall see later, Sword of the Spirit seems to have fallen precisely into this. Second is that one unconsciously (or perhaps even consciously) falls into the modern anti-objective prejudice mentioned above, by which faith is seen as support for a certain kind of moral or social stance.[57]

This second point is vital if we are to understand the charges of manipulation and abuse of conscience that have been raised concerning various covenant communities. Certainly, for a vital Christian faith there must be a warmth of love and vital commitment. However a solid basis of knowledge must lie at its core. Otherwise, the faith cannot become one's own. The martyr—whether one of the victims of Roman persecution or St. Thomas More—dies because he or she simply cannot deny the truth about God. The doctrine of the faith accepted as true, reflected on, studied and embraced as the way things are with God; it becomes a formative factor in the soul. No matter what the world may do and not matter who or how many may apostatize, the individual Christian may truly possess his faith and be supported by it. Bishop Pavol Hnilica, a Jesuit from Slovakia, told how he and his fellow prisoners in a Communist concentration camp were offered their freedom, if only they would accept the Orthodox Patriarch of Moscow as head of the Church and not the Pope. They refused, because this would be to deny the truth about Christ's Church. Thomas More died because, unlike most of the English bishops at the time, he would not profess Henry VIII to be head of the Church in England in opposition to Pope Paul III's universal jurisdiction.

If faith is primarily and essentially a commitment, and indeed a commitment to a community's way of life, then the proper subject of that faith is the community itself, through which the faith is mediated to the member. Indeed, conceived as a commitment to a group and its way of life, faith becomes radically depersonalized. One's entire relationship with God is defined by the group and its leaders. Under such a conception a weakening or questioning of commitment to the group or its leaders (who are the primary and authoritative interpretation of the commitment) is a genuine crisis of faith. If faith *is* the commitment, then one who questions the commitment for any reason has no room left to stand, not even within his own conscience. His faith has no basis for dealing with trials or temptations, since it is not rooted in the intellect. A prominent woman member of The Word of God put this into clear perspective in 1990. Standing before her community, she stated that her Christian life had been a fraud for several years, that the community had taken the place of Christ. As a result, her spiritual life had become increasingly empty and legalistic.

4. The danger of demagoguery

This problem is closely related to the preceding one. Clark is simply too optimistic, too naive in his estimation of the value of "emergent leadership." Such leaders are precisely those best able to get people to do what they want. While the best of them may do great good, the worst can do great harm, unless restrained by institutional bounds. Lyndon B. Johnson, Elon Musk, Nick Fuentes, Charlie Kirk, Adolf Hitler, and St. Paul all possessed most of the characteristics of Clark's emergent leaders. Unless restrained by law, effective oversight, or well-defined authority, such a person can quickly assume a totalitarian role in the lives of others, exploiting them for his own purposes or manipulating them for the sake of the "higher cause." Indeed the growing literature in Protestant circles on the subject of religious abuse points clearly to the danger constituted by pastors and ministers who have gained their position via force of personality and ability to lead others into commitments.[58] Emergent leadership may well be a valuable pastoral resource, but experience and reason show clearly that such leadership must always by subject to and defined by strong institutional authority. Otherwise the danger of demagogic manipulation becomes acute.

C. Bringing It All Together: The Charismatic Renewal

The ideas in *Building Christian Communities* may well have remained largely theoretical were it not for the dramatic outbreak in 1967 of the charismatic renewal. The efforts to found Christian community at Notre Dame through Young Christian Students and Cursillo were foundering, when in the Spring of 1967 news arrived of an astounding event, "too good to be true." A group of students on retreat at Duquesne University had experienced a Pentecostal outpouring of the Holy Spirit, complete with gifts like tongues and prophecy. This experience of the "Baptism in the Holy Spirit" leaped to Notre Dame and a major religious movement was underway.[59] Our purpose here precludes a recounting of the history of this movement. We want here simply to examine the impact of the ideas being developed by Clark and his companions upon this very potent movement and the movement's impact on the ideas.

The outbreak of the charismatic renewal among Catholics was totally unexpected, and as a result the Church had little guidance immediately available for this strange series of events. But as the movement spread like wildfire in those early years, the two things most urgently needed were teaching and guidance. What is this experience about? What should we do with it? The first teachers of the Catholic charismatics were Protestants, especially the Episcopalians and Pentecostals. However, the need for Catholic teaching became clear as the inconsistency of—say—the Pentecostal interpretation of the baptism in the Holy Spirit with the Catholic theology of confirmation became evident. Perhaps even more acute was the problem of direction. Many Protestants, especially the Pentecostals, could not imagine a charismatically renewed Catholic Church, and they fully expected these new Catholic brothers and sisters to have to leave their Church. This issue reached a certain watershed in 1973 as the famous Pentecostal evangelist of New York street gangs, David Wilkerson, published his book, *The Vision*, in which he prophesied that the Pope would reject the Charismatic renewal and "Spirit-filled" Catholics would be forced to leave the Church.

The form that the movement took on very quickly was the local prayer meeting. From about ten to 2,000 people would gather weekly in homes, classrooms, gyms, and parish halls to pray, sing and exercise spiritual gifts. In most cases the hope was that this would catch on, the parish pastor would see the good fruit, and the entire parish would become charismatic. However, the "parish renewal" model never really worked. It simply did not happen, despite efforts of both lay persons and priests. What did "work" and with fairly convincing success were covenant communities.

In South Bend, Indiana—by way of example—some 100 to 150 people met every Wednesday night for a charismatic prayer meeting during 1970 and 1971. Those were successful meetings, marked by fervent prayer, frequent prophecies, conversions and growth. Many who attended this meeting became hungry for something deeper, for the next step, for authentic Christian community. Since the Second Vatican Council there had been much talk about Christian community, and so invigorating were the weekly prayer meetings that they seemed to be a taste of the true unity Christ has in mind for us. Thus the move to community seemed quite natural. One ought to note at this point the strong sense of euphoria that permeated the movement, not only in South Bend, but across the country. It seemed that the Holy Spirit was carrying us along, that all we had to do was to respond to His manifest leadings.

In other words, an *environment* of expectant, vibrant shared faith had been created by the charismatic movement; this was readily interpreted to be the Holy Spirit moving us to a common goal. It only made sense to want a way to regularize, define and solidify this move. For his part, Stephen Clark had already outlined in *Building Christian Communities* a strategy for taking advantage of such an environments to build community. To put it roughly, the theorists at Notre Dame provided a plan for the charismatics, while the movement provided Clark, DeCelles, Martin, and Ranaghan an opportunity. To the charismatics in general it seemed that the Holy Spirit was showing them how to move on. For the Notre Dame theorists, it seemed that God had finally opened a door to create community. On all sides the situation was discussed in terms of "what God is doing."

A further point is to be noted here. For the charismatic movement in general it was necessary to come to grips with the nature and function of the spiritual gifts. Quite naturally, 1 Corinthians 12-14 became very important, as did Romans 12:6-8. Gifts of prophecy, healing, discernment of spirits and the like equipped individual members of the body on occasion to render particular services. In Ephesians 4:11, however, there is another list of gifts, those of "apostles, prophets, pastors, teachers, and evangelists." Unlike the other gifts, these seemed to denote enduring ministries, offices. Indeed they were referred to as the "foundational ministry gifts," and by them the Holy Spirit empowers individuals for leadership roles in the body of Christ. Now just as the true "healer" is recognized by his praying successfully for healings, so the true evangelist or pastor is said to be recognized by winning souls and guiding them successfully to God. The apostle is the one who successfully establishes communities. From the greatest to the least within the charismatic movement, it became common to speak of "the leaders God is raising up for us." Thus did Stephen Clark's emergent leadership find a charismatic-theological basis in the "fivefold foundational ministry gifts" of Ephesians 4:11.

As mentioned above, these were euphoric times in the charismatic movement. We often spoke and heard others speak about how quickly and powerfully God was moving. There was no doubt that great developments were afoot and that for our own sakes and the sake of the Lord's work it was vital to jump in with both feet and be part of what God was doing. And of all the great things that were happening, perhaps most impressive were the communities that were coming into being in Lansing and Ann Arbor, Michigan, in South Bend, in Minneapolis, in Dallas, and in many other places. And on an individual level, each of us was personally caught up and became part of this great work that God was doing. He wants **me** to be a prophet or miracle worker or something similar. I could be God's holy man of faith and power!

But as we have tried to show, these communities were not the pure fruit of a sovereign move of the Holy Spirit. They were the fruit of the combination of some human ideas and a powerful religious movement inspired by God. We now turn our attention to the two main community systems that arose from this. In the following chapters we will look closely at some key aspects of the Sword of the Spirit and the People of Praise. The focus will be on their descriptions of themselves as given in their foundational documents, public teachings and published writings of their founders. By this examination we will show that both Sword of the Spirit and People of Praise are gravely defective, that in their present forms they do not constitute groups in which a Catholic can properly live out his faith and undertake apostolic works.

The approach will be to examine each community according to the following problem areas: 1) covenant and illegitimate ecclesial claims; 2) authority and pastoral care, 3) ecumenism and 4) views on women and marriage. In this context we will also have the chance to examine the important issue of the lack of a theology of grace and the consequent manipulation of consciences from several angles. Since Sword of the Spirit is the more "classical" development of the covenant community model and is in many ways the better defined, we shall consider each of these topics first with respect to Sword of the Spirit and then to People of Praise.

CHAPTER 4.
COVENANT AND ILLEGITIMATE ECCLESIAL CLAIMS

Father W. was concerned. The pastor of a South Bend parish where many members belonged to the People of Praise, he worried about some of the community's teachings and practices, especially those pertaining to marriage and the role of women. He arranged to meet with the head coordinators of the People of Praise to discuss their pastoral practices and teachings with them. As he later confided to this writer, he had expected to be able to come to some mutual understanding with them. Instead he received a polite, somewhat veiled, but clear rebuke. The coordinators of the People of Praise were the shepherds of that body. It was not the place of a parish priest to interfere with their pastoring of their flock. In effect the Catholic pastor stood charged with "sheep stealing."

We have serious reasons to question the ecclesiality of these covenant communities. Their documents and their behavior suggest that they see themselves as much more than renewal groups. Many of their statements put the communities on an equal level with the Church.

A. Sword of the Spirit

The Sword of the Spirit is "an international, ecumenical Christian community of communities that has come together to strengthen the Christian life of its members and to be an instrument of the Lord to establish his reign in the world."[60] Each local body is led by a hierarchically ordered team of *coordinators* (elders) headed by a *senior head coordinator*. Through its senior head coordinator, each such local body of elders is subject to the oversight of the Council, that is of elders from outside the local community. This Council is responsible for the Sword of the Spirit as a whole, and it is seen to have real authority. Sword of the Spirit holds to a certain body of Christian doctrine, namely "the common core of Christian truth ... what all faithful Christians hold in common."[61] It has a well-developed set of teachings, traditional practices and organization of pastoral care. Its leaders have sought to establish relationships of cooperation and understanding with church leaders from several different denominations, but as an organization Sword of the Spirit is subject to no church leader. No local community of it is subject to effective church authority. Sword of the Spirit leaders do visit member communities, however, to teach and form them. Considering all these facts, one can hardly avoid concluding that the Sword of the Spirit is a separate Christian denomination.

What may distinguish Sword of the Spirit from a religious denomination is that many of its members belong to established Christian denominations and churches. A large percentage of its members are Catholic; some of its member communities are entirely Catholic. Since the doctrinal core of Sword of the Spirit has been deliberately constituted of the beliefs common to the mainline Christian churches, one can belong to Sword of the Spirit without having to deny the tenants of his Catholic faith. Concerning this the Charter of Sword of the Spirit further states:

> The Sword of the Spirit is a missionary body, committed to spreading the Gospel and to strengthening God's people throughout the world.

> The Sword of the Spirit as a body does not claim the authority of a Christian church ... it desires to strengthen Christian churches and fellowships, not to compete with them.

In spite of these disclaimers, the Sword of the Spirit looks so much like a church that we must be concerned. Its purposes, to strengthen the Christian life of its members, to spread the Gospel and "to be an instrument of God to establish his reign in the world," are the purposes of the Church. Its structure as a "community of communities" parallels that of the Catholic Church. We have, therefore, *prima facie* reason to suspect that Sword of the Spirit is nothing other than a Christian denomination which allows its members to participate in the activities of other Christian denominations. Further light is shed on this important issue by a close examination of the Sword of the Spirit covenant and its understanding of community. We will see that, in fact, Sword of the Spirit does effectively claim for itself the status of a church.

The opening paragraph of the Sword of the Spirit covenant is so rich in startling, theologically important claims that it is worth quoting in full.[62]

> (1) God has invited us to enter a covenant with Him. (2) He has offered to be our God and has called us to be His people. (3) In a special way, as members of The Sword of the Spirit, He has brought us into the New Covenant established by his Son, Jesus. (4) He has formed us into a people for Himself and has confirmed and further revealed His call to us by giving us this name, The Sword of the Spirit.

The first sentence explicitly claims a divine origin for the Sword of the Spirit covenant. It has been offered on God's initiative. Sentences 1, 2, and 4 clearly echo the covenant between Yahweh and the people of Israel.[63] The allusions of the Mosaic covenant in Scripture are unmistakable. One might be tempted to dismiss this phrasing as a charismatic oversimplification or exaggeration (How often does one hear "God told me ..." or "God did this ..." in charismatic circles?). However, the context here requires us to take this expression seriously. The authors of this covenant are theologically literate, careful in their speech, and well-known for nuancing their public statements. Furthermore, this initiative—this divine intervention—has precisely those effects that only a divine work could have: a people *is* called into being, formed by God and named as "God's people."

If this statement is true, then God's covenant with The Sword of the Spirit is a major event in salvation history. God has raised up a new people within the Church to be a people distinctively his own. The claim being made here goes far beyond the claims of St. Benedict, St. Francis of Assisi, St. Ignatius or of any other founder of a religious community within the Church. Here there is a very real question of a new revelation, of a substantive addition to the deposit of faith and a major change in the structure of Christ's Church. The addition is not, on the face of it, doctrinal but ecclesiological. It is stated that God has raised up a new people, one not spoken of in the Scriptures, a people that is within but not identical with his Church. And yet he has already established the Church as one, holy, Catholic and apostolic to be the sacrament of unity for all men.[64]

The second sentence heightens the difficulty by relating this Sword of the Spirit covenant to this New Covenant. One is "brought into the New Covenant" by baptism, through which we are buried with Christ and rise with him.[65] "Baptism symbolizes and brings about a mystical but real incorporation into the crucified and glorious body of Christ."[66] Furthermore, by our participation in the Eucharist and reception of Holy Communion, we enter fully into the New Covenant. Indeed, no more complete or perfect participation in the New Covenant can be conceived. What, then, is the point of asserting that through the Sword of the Spirit, "He has brought us into the New Covenant"? The point appears to be that the covenant of the Sword of the Spirit enables its members to enter into the New Covenant not merely as individuals, but as a distinct people. Thus the covenant later states: "We desire to consecrate our lives to Him not simply as individuals but as members of a people, members of the Sword of the Spirit." In other words, as a Catholic, one is a Christian "individualistically"; within Sword of the Spirit, one enters the New Covenant as part of a people. Such a conception strikes at the essential unity of the Church and amounts to a denial of a true Catholic solidarity.

Now, without a doubt, it can be urged—as Clark himself has in *Building Christian Communities* —that many parishes look today more like service institutions than authentic communities. And, to be sure, many Catholics may well be living out their faith in an unduly private manner. Nonetheless, *we cannot accept the Sword of the Spirit covenant as valid or truthful without denying the unity that is an essential mark of the Church.* We must recall that the Church herself is an ordered society—indeed a "perfect society"—united under one Vicar of Christ. In each part of the earth the faithful are gathered around their bishops as a community (not just "technically"[67] but really).[68] And as they gather to celebrate the Eucharist they are really united with Christ as He offers His perfect sacrifice to the Father. In receiving the sacrament of the altar, each of the faithful, intimately united in love with Christ, is also joined to his brothers and sisters. This unity, let us emphasize, is real. Ways may be proposed to help Catholics become more aware of it or to live it out more perfectly, but these must build on the ontological reality, the unity which Christ has already established.

What then is this people, Sword of the Spirit? How is it one? With these questions we turn to the issue of community. Stephen Clark's definition from *Building* Christian *Communities* is helpful, though not the final word.

"A basic Christian community is an environment of Christians which can provide for the basic needs of its members to live the Christian life."[69] There follows a list of those basic needs; interestingly, none of them has to do with the sacraments. This environment of Christians is centered around Christ as its central value and organizing principle. Indeed, as Clark clearly recognizes, the community must, in some clear sense, present the whole Christ both to its members and to the outside world. The community, as the body of Christ, must, in a way, BE Christ to the world.

Clark's understanding of community permeates his other published works. According to this understanding, community is the place where one can most securely discern God's will by receiving direction from Christian leaders.[70] The most complete statement of this vision is *Patterns of Christian Community* edited by Stephen B. Clark, but largely the product of coordinators' meetings within The Word of God Community.

The reader of *Patterns of Christian Community* is struck by how very much the book has to do with leaders, leadership structures and the exercise of authority. In effect, *Patterns of Christian Community* describes a totalitarian (or totalist) structure in which all life, all wisdom and all unity come from the leaders, whose authority extends in principle over the entire life of each member. Lest this claim appear too extreme, the following should be noted:

- Though tolerated, disagreement within the community is carefully regulated. Specifically a member may express his disagreement to those over him and then on "up through channels." If the leadership does not accept his point then he is to try to reconcile himself to their view. In any case, he is not to take his disagreement to other members of the community and certainly not to anyone outside.[71]
- Likewise, appeals concerning decisions, whether corporate or personal, may only go upward through the

community hierarchy and certainly not to someone outside.

- Normally the member obeys his leaders, expecting them to lead him into God's will.
- They (i.e., members of the community) should receive a personal reproof or judgment by their governor as something that they are committed to accept, and either obey or, if they have a serious reservation appeal to the governor who is over their governor ... They should respond to them willingly and with thankfulness for the help they are being given.[72]
- The elders receive their authority from the Lord and are answerable to him.[73]

The notion that an impulse to greater holiness or a fundamental correction could come from a non-governor within the group—or that a "prophetic" element within the community might be right and the leaders wrong—is absent from *Patterns of Christian Community*. Indeed, the leaders believe that such a situation cannot arise if everything is functioning properly.[74]

The central importance of the leaders of the community is perhaps best revealed by a comment cited earlier from Stephen Clark's *Unordained Elders and Renewal Communities*. There Clark is addressing the issue of bishops appointing clerical leaders for such communities. He states: "Not to respect the autonomy of a community in the choice of its leaders is to destroy the community or to absorb it into another."[75] But the "other community" in question here is the Church itself. In other words, even for the bishop to impose leadership on a community is to change the fundamental character of the Christian community. This is nothing short of an implicit claim that the community is by rights independent of the Church.

Now to be sure, the Second Vatican Council is careful to provide for the protection of the respective charisms of various communities (i.e., religious orders). A bishop ought not to insist that the Capuchins in his diocese teach in his Catholic schools, for example. On the other hand, Pope John Paul II did feel free to install someone of his own choosing as General of the Jesuits after Fr. Pedro Arrupe retired. Although many people complained about this move, no one suggested that the Pope had changed the fundamental character of the Society of Jesus.

The essential point here goes far beyond the question of a religious order's charism. A fundamental issue is at stake: the nature of community itself. According to Clark's theory, the covenant community is autonomous in relation to larger outside groupings. This claimed autonomy seems a bit puzzling at first, since in *Patterns of Christian Community* and the actual structure of Sword of the Spirit include provisions for accountability to authorities from outside the local community. Clark's remark, then, suggests that (1) the leaders must come from within and be recognized by the organically structured local body and (2) any outside authority or accountability should not be merely administrative in nature but rather communitarian and directly related to the local community. Furthermore, the leadership of the local community is by its nature non-apostolic. To be sure, Clark allows for and even favors the ordination of community leaders. Nevertheless their true authority as elders flows not from ordination but from their having emerged organically as the leaders of this community.

Here we must note specifically Clark's idea that the Catholic Church is fundamentally a service and administrative institution rather than a community or a people.[76] He argues that the bishopric and presbyterate in the Catholic Church today function more like service institutions. The goal of renewing the faith life of the Church is abandoned in favor of establishing something entirely new. Thus, those communities cannot be true renewal organizations, but rather replacements for present Church institutions. In this, the true nature of the Catholic Church as the People of God as an organic, ordered society is effectively denied.

The fundamental value and the organizing principle—the point, if you will—of the Christian Community is Jesus Christ himself. We need to ask, then, how is Christ present in or to the Christian community, as Sword of the Spirit understands it. This is a particularly difficult task, since Sword of the Spirit does not have a well-developed spirituality. Teachings on holiness are generally restricted to the exhortations to pray faithfully every day, read the Scriptures and serve the brethren. No attempt is made to explain how God works in the soul. It is simply accepted that the Holy Spirit moves in the heart of the faithful Christian. In the final analysis, the community serves as the principal agent of grace in the lives of its members. By living the life of the community and obeying its patterns one is formed as a Christian. Clark writes: "In Christianity, institutions have to be looked at as secondary, because the primary thing which changes people (makes them Christians, makes them better or worse Christians) is the effect of environments."[77] According to this view, the primary locus of Christ's presence is the community itself.[78]

Clark makes this teaching explicit in his *Man and Woman in Christ* where he states that the purpose of Jesus's work of redemption was "the creation of a people, a social body living a way of life that reflects God's own nature."[79] According to Clark, the New Testament is to be read primarily from the perspective of this social structure.[80] This structure is a people that acts as Christ and has the character of Christ. In fact, the goal of this people and of each community that makes it up is to be **one person**, and that person is Christ.[81]

Let us dwell on this point. The Scriptures speak of the Church as "a body" and as the "Body of Christ." St. Paul writes (in Ephesians 4) of the community being built up into that "one perfect man" who is Christ. But the Scriptures do not speak of the Church or the community as "one person." The distinction is important. The point of the analogy of the body is that a genuine unity can exist in a whole, even if the parts have disparate functions. And the "one new man" which is the community is a unity animated by the Holy Spirit as by a soul. Neither of these concepts, however, cancels the integrity or autonomy of the individual. The term "person" signifies one subsistent being. The parts of a person are only parts and have no autonomy of their own; only the person has personality. If the community is truly "one person," then the individual member is seriously out of order if he initiates anything other than what the head (as seat of intelligence and will) desires or permits. He is like a withered hand or a leg with an uncontrollable twitch—except, of course, that he is responsible for his deviant behavior. Precisely this is one root of the problem that has led to persistent charges of authoritarianism. The most significant point to note here is that, in Clark's view, Christ is present to the world and the community neither in any one person nor sacramentally, but rather through the activity of the community. The people which manifests a godly character is Christ's presence; indeed, it is the very person of Christ.

We are now in a position to conclude that the Sword of the Spirit is based on a seriously flawed ecclesiology, one that deviates decisively from that of the Catholic Church. By claiming to be the Body of Christ (indeed, the *person* of Christ) and to stand in a unique covenant relationship with the Lord, one in which it is a distinctive people, the Sword of the Spirit has actually arrogated to itself the status of the Church. In and of itself, this is a grave problem, and existentially it is the root of many abuses. We shall further unfold the flaws of this subsequently as we consider the issues of pastoring and ecumenism.

As we turn to an examination of the covenant and ecclesial claims of the People of Praise, it may be helpful to reflect on an event that happened in the People of Praise, but which also dramatically illustrates the fundamental flaw embraced by both communities in their understanding of the spiritual life. Sue was the mother of a severely disabled daughter whose life was drawing to a close. Indeed, the girl was close to death, but there was to be a weekend retreat for the women of the People of Praise. All the women were expected to attend. On the Saturday of the retreat, Sue headed off to St. Patrick's church for the morning Mass and to spend some time in prayer. Then she headed over to the LaSalle Building where the community had its headquarters and retreat facilities—a walk of about six blocks. Having arrived late, that is, after the retreat had started, Sue was confronted by the handmaid who was leading the retreat. Granted that Sue might reasonably want to attend Mass at such an important time for her family, she should nevertheless have joined her sisters in community for the retreat. After all, her sisters were committed to supporting her in her difficulties. She was wrong to have taken a different way to deal with her problems. Her sisters would have ministered to her, and Sue would have received important teaching about her role as a woman of the People of Praise.

B. The People of Praise

Like Sword of the Spirit, the People of Praise exists as a network of local communities sharing common teaching and practices under a single authority that is both administrative and pastoral. In this the People of Praise also looks very much like a church denomination, and we must ask to what extent this organization arrogates to itself claims proper to the Church.

The People of Praise covenant differs significantly from that of the Sword of the Spirit. Although the People of Praise has based its understanding of covenant on the Scriptural model, it does not claim that God is party to the covenant. The covenant itself affirms: "We covenant ourselves to live our lives together in Christ our Lord by the power of his Spirit. We agree to become a Christian community." The constitution of the People of Praise states explicitly that the covenant is an agreement among human beings; it is a "contract."[82] Consonant with this understanding, People of Praise coordinator and spokesman Dan DeCelles asserts that the requirement that one be released from the covenant before leaving the community is really just a matter of courtesy or common human decency. "It was a two-way agreement at the beginning. It seems reasonable that it should be two-way at the end."[83] While this is a peculiarly stringent understanding of human agreements (otherwise one's fiancée could never unilaterally break off the engagement, or a member could never resign from the country club), it poses no theological problem as such.

However, in light of these definitions and Mr. DeCelles's statement, certain other authoritative pronouncements and policies become extremely puzzling. When a number of covenanted members left the community as a group in the late 1970s, Kevin Ranaghan gave a teaching attributing their behavior to a specific demon called a "quitting spirit." By their behavior, these people had manifested their own "quitting spirits," and this was compared to the attitudes of those who abandon their commitments to marriage or the priesthood. "Covenant breaking is like adultery. It really is," he taught. "But covenanted members are not free. The covenant establishes a permanent family relationship. ... It's really very similar to marriage. It's permanent; therefore it's different."[84] On another occasion about three years later, Overall Coordinator Paul DeCelles was explaining the departure from the community covenant by a married couple. The wife had been advised by her doctor that remaining in northern Indiana would seriously endanger her health. Yet DeCelles taught his community that even under such circumstances, the coordinators must be very cautious in releasing members from the covenant. This is an astonishing claim of authority. In the case just mentioned, the community members were immigrants from Communist Poland. The husband had been held for five years in a Nazi POW camp. And yet, having faced the great evils of Nazism and Communism, he was incompetent to know what was best for his wife without discernment from the coordinators. The doctor's recommendation might well be an attack "from the Enemy" to weaken the community. In my own case, as I was seriously reassessing my own membership in the community, I told a head coordinator, Kevin Ranaghan, that I felt that I could no longer be true to myself if I remained in the People of Praise. He answered, "How can you speak of being true to yourself when you are thinking about breaking one of the core commitments of your life?"

Similarly, in an article in *New Heaven/New Earth*, Paul DeCelles identifies the quitting spirit as worse even than sensuality or unchastity. "Sexual impurity is not the biggest threat to Christian character today. Unfaithfulness is. Quitting is. ... A quitting spirit is the poison of modern mankind."[85] The thrust of these teachings is plainly theological and spiritual; to break the covenant is in some way to be unfaithful to God. Another pronouncement appears in the People of Praise internal newsletter, *Vine and Branches*, May 1992. There Clem Walters (a senior coordinator) affirms that the Overall Coordinator may refuse to release a member from the covenant for that member's own good. The reason is that in the covenant there is seen to be a "spiritual protection" which it is important not to lose. The member—even though he may have chosen to leave the community on the basis of his own free decision—is not regarded as free to leave; to do so is to expose himself to spiritual dangers from which only the community can protect him.

Such statements, together with the People of Praise's actual practices when a member does seek to leave, clearly imply that the community believes its covenant to have a spiritual status beyond that of any agreement among human beings alone. We must ask how this covenant comes to provide spiritual covering and why leaving it is evidence of demonic activity. Typically, the People of Praise does not attempt a theological basis for its claims about itself. In this respect it differs significantly from Sword of the Spirit. We might say that while Sword of the Spirit is ideological, the People of Praise is empiricist or pragmatic. Of course this makes a theological critique more difficult. Nevertheless, an understanding of this apparent conflict is possible. We begin to find this answer in Paul DeCelles's article cited above.

The true evil of a "quitting spirit" is that it can lead one to break his promises to God, and, DeCelles observes, this is worse even than adultery. We may infer then that even though the covenant is in the first place an agreement among human beings, it also constitutes a promise or commitment to God, for the second sentence reads: "We agree to become a Christian community." By committing themselves directly to one another, members also agree to build something for God's sake. The spiritual effect and value of the covenant derives from the fact that it founds a Christian community. Even if the People of Praise refrains from attributing divine origin to its covenant, it clearly attributes spiritual weight and authority to the community itself. Our focus, then, must be on the understanding of the community.

After stating the intention to form a "Christian community," the People of Praise covenant goes on to specify what that community is. Within it members will find "the essential core of (their) life in the Spirit, in worship and the sacraments, in spiritual and moral guidance, in service and apostolic activity." The covenant expresses the expectation that the Holy Spirit will guide the community, especially through the "foundational ministry gifts of apostles, prophets, pastors, teachers, and evangelists." (cf. Ephesians 4:11) By it the community members accept responsibility for meeting all one another's needs, including the spiritual. These specifications do describe a true Christian community. The point, however, is that the People of Praise claims that simply by making this covenant, such a community has come into being. "As a way of participating in this new covenant in Christ, the covenant of the People of Praise establishes a Christian community."[86] The issue is to determine whether this is true.

In an important article, "Not every 'Community' Is Really Community,"[87] Paul DeCelles addresses this issue squarely. Noting that we often use words imprecisely—in this case "community" —and that this imprecision causes confusion and misunderstanding, he proposes to present the criteria for a Christian community in the full, true, proper sense of the term. Like many other religious leaders who have defined "community," he takes Acts 2:42-46 as his key text. He then proceeds to analyze this text to determine the three essential characteristics of any true Christian community. These are "meetings, teachings and life together." What is significant about DeCelles analysis is not so much what he says as what he omits.

In verse 42 of the text, St. Luke refers to the "fellowship and teaching of the Apostles" and to "the breaking of the bread." Without arguing the point, DeCelles uncritically assumes that "apostles" equals "leader of the community" and that whoever leads the community is *ipso facto* an apostle.[88] But this is not so. An apostle was one of the Twelve appointed by Christ or—in the case of Matthias—the other apostles, to rule His Church. Today, the title apostle properly applies only to the bishops in the Catholic and Orthodox Churches. Therefore, by DeCelles' own standard, only that is properly called a community which is headed by a bishop. However, he fails to recognize this.

This point about the meaning of the term 'apostle' is not idle, as a further consideration of the terms "fellowship" and "breaking of the bread" reveals. Joseph Ratzinger argues that the "fellowship" (koinonia) referred to here is the Eucharistic assembly, that is, the brotherhood of those joined in Christ's sacrifice on the altar and by having consumed His Body and Blood.[89] This assembly is, of course, led by one ordained to offer that sacrifice *in persona Christi*. But the key phrase that DeCelles completely misses is "the breaking of the bread," which John Paul II has called a "technical term" for the Eucharist.[90] The pope has used this very text to insist that the Eucharist is essential to the unity of Christ's followers. Indeed by this sacrament we enjoy today the same mark of unity that characterized the early Church. "It is an essential truth, not only of doctrine but also of life, that the Eucharist builds the Church as the authentic community of the People of God ... *bearing the same mark of unity that was shared by the apostles and first disciples of the Lord.*" (emphasis added)[91]

Thus by his own strict standards, properly applied, DeCelles's communal organization is not a true Christian community. As we have already seen, such an organization cannot be the body of Christ. Why, then, do DeCelles and his followers continue to claim that their group is an authentic Christian community? This may stem partly from a simple failure to study theology, especially ecclesiology, in depth. But there is a deeper answer, one that explains even the failure to take theology seriously.

Like Sword of the Spirit, the People of Praise is a system of tangible grace. Unity is something experienced in the gatherings, and its ontological status is not examined. Through the coordinators' teachings the members experience a confident, authoritative proclamation. In their various services and activities, they experience the love of the brethren and so on. The people in church on Sunday may all be strangers, but in the community household, love is shared on the "nitty-gritty" level. For every essential element in the life of the Church there is an experiential element within People of Praise corresponding to it. Thus one deeply immersed in its life may very well never see a need for a critical theological reflection, because he manifestly experiences it all. For the member, life in the People of Praise may well offer his richest experience of Christian community. Therefore to him it must be authentic. It is ***experienced as*** the body of Christ; therefore it must *be* the body of Christ. The first year or so in community is usually so different from ordinary life[92] and so powerful an experience of communion that the new member feels himself to be living an authentic New Testament Christianity.

Like the Church, the People of Praise requires that its members contribute to its support. All members are required to contribute at least 5% of their gross income to the community.[93] Senior coordinator Kevin Ranaghan encourages community members to increase this amount by 1% annually for five years to reach a total of 10%, in addition to their contributions to the "sharing fund" and Trinity School. This community support contribution is an obligation prior to and independent of one's parish contribution, because the *community* is the "essential core" of the member's life in the Spirit.

The People of Praise (like the Sword of the Spirit) has a celibate "brotherhood" and "sisterhood" consisting of young men and women who consecrate themselves to a lifetime of being "single for the Lord." The *Pastoral Guidelines* give explicit instructions to heads concerning leading members into this kind of life. However, no mention is made of either the priesthood or life in a canonical religious order.[94] As one would expect, the People of Praise has produced very few vocations to the priesthood or religious life, although one member, Peter Smith was ordained and even elevated to the episcopate as Auxiliary Bishop of Portland.

Like Sword of the Spirit, the People of Praise attributes divine origin to itself. The Holy Spirit purportedly called the community into being as a people for the praise of God. Thus *"Because Our Lord loves us, he pours out his Spirit on us so that we might be his People of Praise."*[95] The invitation to join originates with God; it is a vocation. *"Those who make the covenant are making a definitive and permanent choice of a particular mode of life lived in response to an invitation by the Spirit of the Lord."*[96] The People of Praise's most important ecclesial claims, however, are those written directly into its covenant. This states that the "essential core" of one's life in the Spirit is to be found in the People of Praise, and this core is further described as "worship and the sacraments, spiritual and moral guidance, prayer and apostolic activity." This is a very strong claim. By purporting to offer this "essential core" the People of Praise claims implicitly to be the means, the society by which Christ saves its members, and this is what the Church is. But let us now focus on this phrase "worship and the sacraments."

The term "worship" can be understood in two related ways. The first concerns the activity of prayer. The People of Praise does make prayer a high priority. Members are encouraged to pray, and the group as a whole prays during part of its assemblies. In fact, as its name suggests, prayer and worship—especially the prayer of praising God—is to be the point of the People of Praise: "Prayer and prayer meetings are basic to our life. Through regular opportunities for personal prayer, small-group prayer, community prayer and liturgical prayer, we become who we are—People of Praise."[97] At one community gathering in 1974, Kevin Ranaghan prophesied to the community that the Lord was calling the People of Praise into being because although "there are many people who worship me, and there are many who pray to me, there are only a few who praise me." This is a curious prophecy, because at the time Ranaghan was a doctoral student in theology at Notre Dame, working on a dissertation in liturgical studies. He surely knew that at the beginning of every day, the Church prays "Lauds", that is "Morning Praise", which begins, "Lord, open my lips, and my mouth will proclaim your praise." Throughout the community's life, attention has been devoted to fostering worship in the community, especially through developing a strong "music ministry."

Worship in the People of Praise gatherings typically takes the form of a well-regulated charismatic prayer meeting. That is, there are songs, spontaneous prayer in English, prayer in tongues and singing in tongues, as well as charismatic gifts woven together under the direction of the leader (always a coordinator). For the individual member, this is ordinarily vocal spontaneous prayer.

Such prayer is undoubtedly a good thing. However, we must be careful in characterizing it as worship. The standard criterion and ultimate instance of any act of Christian worship must be Christ's perfect act of worship when He offered His own life to the Father on the Cross. That is, worship has the aspect of sacrifice as well as vocal prayer. Paul DeCelles has recognized this and has taught the community that the shedding of blood is an essential part of a covenant. In the People of Praise this shedding consists of the willingness, expressed in the covenant, of each member to lay down his lifeblood for the others and for the body as a whole. Indeed, the covenant of the People of Praise is regarded as the gift of their lifeblood to God.[98] Thus it is an act of worship. In short, the worship offered by the People of Praise is more than the prayers offered at its various gatherings; rather it is the gift of their corporate and individual lifeblood offered through their covenant. Importantly, this gift of one's lifeblood is not salvific. Christ's shedding of his blood is.

When we consider this in relationship to Christ's own sacrifice of worship—the sacrifice that establishes the New Covenant—we see that the worship of the People of Praise is gravely defective. Ninety-five percent of People of Praise members are Roman Catholic, including much of its top leadership. As such they can and do enter into Christ's perfect sacrifice at every Mass they attend. When they receive Communion, they are joined to the suffering Christ as He gives Himself to the Father. In this Communion, their own gift of self is transformed by being joined to Christ and is thus perfected. The Eucharist is thus the essence and the heart of Christian worship. Catholics may certainly offer true worship outside the celebration of the Eucharist; a charismatic prayer meeting can be genuinely worshipful. However, such worship is always rooted in the Eucharist, even if indirectly. In private and group devotions, the Catholic prays from the Eucharist, from which his prayer derives as a kind of overflow. Every private prayer is, as it were, an expression of love, gratitude and recommitment following the last Eucharist and a preparation and yearning for the next. The devout soul who whispers "I love you, Jesus!" in his room is speaking to the one with whom he was intimately united last Sunday. And when he prays "Come into my heart and fill it," he does so knowing that soon he will indeed receive his Savior sacramentally. In fact, insofar as it relates in some way to Christ's gift of himself at the Last Supper and on Calvary, *any* Christian's prayer is founded on the Eucharist through participation. What this means is that the Catholic Church is the "priestly people" because it is the Eucharistic people.[99] Conversely, the People of Praise is not because it is not Eucharistic.

My point is this: The Catholic who approaches the Lord as a member of the People of Praise, that is as offering his own lifeblood through the People of Praise covenant, does so wrongly. In effect, he takes a step backward by subsuming his prayer under the imperfect covenant of this group rather than the perfect covenant made by Christ on Calvary and renewed at every Mass. Unfortunately, some members honestly believe that the intimacy they enjoy with Christ by virtue of their membership in the community is greater than that which any Catholic enjoys in Holy Communion.

This is not mere quibbling with words. To join one's worship with that of the crucified Christ in the Eucharist is to accept the cross in one's own life. Whoever loves Christ enough to enter fully into this sacrifice will indeed experience the Cross. But this will come as Christ allows it and as the Christian freely embraces it. For the community member, however, the "cross" is well defined by the People of Praise pattern of life, and he embraces it by living that life wholeheartedly and completely. The sacrifice represented by making the covenant of the People of Praise is taken seriously. One "lays down his life" according to the requirements of the community—by faithfully attending men's and women's groups, submitting to one's head willingly, performing four hours of service to the community every week, contributing 5-13% of one's gross income to the community,[100] and so on.

In the light of all this it is clear that the life of the People of Praise as such is not centered on the sacraments but on the community as such. Nevertheless, in contrast to Sword of the Spirit, the People of Praise does explicitly acknowledge the role of the sacraments, albeit to a limited extent. Specifically the leaders of the People of Praise have stressed the fact that in Baptism one is objectively united to Christ, and Paul DeCelles has taught that this is the sacramental basis of the People of Praise—the fact that every member is really joined to Christ through Baptism.[101] The community does require that anyone seeking Baptism receive the Sacrament in an established Church and not just as a member of People of Praise. It is worth noting that since both DeCelles and Ranaghan are ordained permanent deacons, they can "have their cake and eat it too." Many community members have their weddings and baptisms performed by the community leaders.

Regarding the other sacraments, however, the People of Praise is ambivalent. The community professes to find within its fellowship "the essential core of our life in the Spirit," including the sacraments, but as an ecumenical group it cannot celebrate all the sacraments together. In 1985 Paul DeCelles gave a formal videotaped teaching on the covenant to the entire People of Praise. In this he attempted to explain the community's position concerning the sacraments thus: "To the extent that any of our denominational churches have the sacraments, to that extent we all wish we could share them." With such blatant denominational relativism, the sacraments are reduced to objects of wishing. In the section on "Holiness" in *The Spirit and the Purpose of the People of Praise*, the subject is treated as follows:

> The community fosters this heart-knowledge in many ways, and has built into its way of life many opportunities for prayer—and for enrichment through the sacraments in accord with the disciplines of our various churches and denominations. These practices, traditionally honored in the church, are honored in the People of Praise.[102]

Such a manner of speaking about the sacraments is very curious. One could speak meaningfully of enrichment through icons (Eastern Church), the rosary (Western Church), and Protestant-style preaching, and we can honor such forms of devotion. Unfortunately, the Rosary, which the Catholic Church has warmly recommended for centuries and continues to do so, has been strongly discouraged in the People of Praise, except for strictly private recitation. These devotions are creations of human culture—devotional practices developed by human beings in response to God's grace and inspired by the Holy Spirit. But the sacraments come directly from God; they are "instituted by Christ to give grace." Or as Pope John Paul II put it, a sacrament is "a *sign that* efficaciously *transmits in the visible world the invisible mystery hidden in God from eternity.*"[103]

It is very easy today to fall into the trap of regarding Mass and the seven Sacraments as if the Catholic Church devised them for its members. In fact, they are the means by which Christ himself has chosen to sanctify all men. Although God in his mercy will forgive any repentant sinner, the way He has established to forgive the sins of the baptized is sacramental confession. Likewise his body is real food and his blood is real drink, and without them one cannot have real life. Holy Orders is how Christ conforms men to himself so that they can act effectively in His name and person for the sanctification of others. "Through that sacrament priests, by the anointing of the Holy Spirit, are ... configured to Christ the Priest in such a way that they are able to work in the person of

Christ the Head."[104] They are far more than devotions for the enrichment of our personal heart-knowledge. The sacraments are intended by Christ to be absolutely essential for our life in Him. To speak of merely "honoring" them is to misconstrue completely what sacraments are all about.

In the analysis of Sword of the Spirit, we noted the claim that the individual community stands as autonomous vis-à-vis the Church, and we described this autonomy. We see a very similar stance by the People of Praise, although this community does attempt to see itself as at the service of the church. In the community's newsletter, *Vine and Branches*, Paul DeCelles has repeatedly addressed the question of "meaningful church oversight." Some of DeCelles's remarks in this regard are especially revealing.

In an interview in the April 1991 issue of *Vine and Branches*, DeCelles was asked about the need for such oversight as a safeguard against the community's going astray, becoming heretical or developing into a cult. DeCelles said that since People of Praise teaches no new doctrine, heresy is not a danger; their "openness to the world" is a safeguard against cult behavior. He then addresses the issue of church oversight in the following exchange:

> V&B: Wouldn't it help if we came under the oversight of some church group or groups?
>
> Paul: Personally, I don't think submitting the community to an **outside body** is the best safeguard against becoming isolated. Some groups have tried that and have still ended up pretty peculiar. For the kind of community we are, I think the kind of openness I've described is better. (emphasis added)[105]

Now this presumes precisely the premise that Clark accepts in *Unordained Elders*, when he argues that an external authority ought not appoint a community's leaders, and its implications are damning. As a Catholic (indeed, an ordained deacon) whose community is predominantly Catholic, DeCelles is clearly referring to Roman Catholic bishops here and it follows necessarily that he regards that Church as an "outside body." However the truth is that this "outside body" is the Body of Christ. The strictly logical consequence of DeCelles assertion is that the People of Praise is independent of and separate from the Church of Christ.

So too, in the August 1992 issue DeCelles remarked that the Catholic bishops where the two largest People of Praise branches are located have declined to be involved in the community's pastoral care. They want Catholic members to receive pastoral care through their own parishes. DeCelles seems to take this to mean that these bishops are happy to let the People of Praise go their way, but this is not so. An appropriate response by DeCelles would be to disband the community's pastoral structure or strive to integrate it with and submit it to local pastors in those dioceses. In that same article, DeCelles implies that it is up to Church officials to inquire if they want further information or involvement with the People of Praise.

The thrust of all this is that the Catholic Church and its dioceses are simply other religious organizations—larger than but more or less on a par with the People of Praise—that stand in no organic relationship with the local community of Christians. It is very important to note that nowhere in the People of Praise foundational documents is it stated or suggested that the People of Praise falls under any authority within the Church.[106] Indeed, at the end of an important three-day meeting of the entire community in June 1983, Paul DeCelles briefly described the nature and mission of the People of Praise: "We are the body of Christ, and our mission is to renew the face of the earth."[107] In 1993, during a formal teaching on authority in the community, DeCelles stated: "The purpose of the People of Praise, because we're a Christian community, is fundamentally to hold our lives in common in order to love God and to love one another as Christ has loved us."[108] These are fundamentally descriptions of the Church itself, and not of a renewal community within it.

The only relationship with the Church as such exists on the part of the individual People of Praise member. The People of Praise policy concerning participation in parish activities reflects the priority of the community. Members may serve in their parishes as liturgical "ministers" or on various committees or boards, provided such service does not conflict with community service or meetings. A fairly large number of community members have served as Eucharistic ministers and lectors. Fewer undertake services that require a significant time investment.

Although some of the community's top leadership (most notably Kevin Ranaghan) have participated in national and international charismatic renewal leadership organizations, ordinary members are not to take such prominent roles. One member who was appointed to serve on the Pontifical Council of the Laity was dismissed from the community for having taken a "high profile" position. An interesting—and revealing—episode in the secular realm arose with Dr. Amy Coney Barrett's appointment as a judge on the federal bench in 2017. Until that moment, her name had occasionally appeared in the community newsletter, *Vine and the Branches*. After this high-profile presidential appointment, references to Judge Barrett disappeared from that newsletter.

The individual community member is strongly discouraged from relying on the Church for his spiritual formation. At one point my wife brought some worries about the community to confession. Subsequently, we invited the coordinator of our branch to visit us and address some of Marie's concerns in the light of the priest's counsel to her. This coordinator was visibly displeased and admonished her that in confession, she should "confess her sins, get absolution and get out." Confession was not a place to talk about her life in the community. Several community members and former community members have since testified that they have been given the same instructions.

The autonomy implicitly claimed here finds its basis in the foundational documents of the community. Both the covenant as well as *Spirit and Purpose* state that the headship of the People of Praise rests on the "foundational ministry gifts of apostles, pastors, prophets, teachers, and evangelists." In its discussion of authority in the People of Praise, *the Spirit and Purpose* cites Hebrews 13:17, "Obey your leaders and submit to them; for they are keeping watch over your souls, as men who will have to give account," and further citing 2 Timothy 4:2, "Those in authority for the community should 'preach the word, be urgent in season and out of season, convince, rebuke, and exhort, be unfailing in patience and in teaching'." These Scripture texts refer to the authority of bishops, not to lay leaders of a voluntary religious group. In point of fact, the leaders of the People of Praise have claimed for themselves none less than apostolic authority. Indeed, *The Spirit and Purpose* states concerning the Overall Coordinator: "He is the visible principle of unity of the whole community."[109] This is almost precisely how the Catholic Church describes its bishops and the Pope.[110] According to the *Principles of Structure and Government of the People of Praise*,[111] this man is the "proper superior" of every member of the community. According to Vatican II, the pope "enjoys supreme, full, immediate, and universal authority over the care of souls".[112] Yet, we do not hear of the Pope telling people whether or not they should move to the Southwest for one's health or directing a husband when to allow his wife to nap. The Pope may issue an encyclical on the use of contraceptives[113], but neither he nor a parish priest will interfere in a couple's family planning decisions, much less concerning their courtship and marriage. Such things have happened frequently in several covenant communities. In sum, the foundational documents of the People of Praise clearly assert that the community's leaders enjoy objective apostolic and pastoral authority from the Lord himself—authority modeled on but independent of the Church's pastors. Thus like Sword of the Spirit, the People of Praise claims to be autonomous with respect to the Church.

C. Implications for Faith

Both Sword of the Spirit and People of Praise arrogate to themselves the place of the Church in the faith lives of their members. Both community systems describe themselves as a specific means to respond to and live out the New Covenant. This has a powerful and ultimately destructive effect on those who enter these communities. We do well to consider how and why this is so.

Very few members joined the People of Praise or Sword of the Spirit out of weakness. It is a mistake to see these groups as populated with dysfunctional misfits looking for sure answers to uncertain times and a firm guiding hand through a perilous world. Rather, they are usually highly motivated and idealistic, wanting a deeper life of faith for themselves and an opportunity to serve Christ and the Gospel more completely.[114] The covenant community offers not only a powerful experience of the Christian life, but also a concrete way to live out a total consecration.

Very few community members would consider leaving the Catholic Church. Indeed, many join these communities hoping to help renew the Church. An additional characteristic is that most members have been active in or influenced by the charismatic renewal. Therefore, they expect their faith to have a strong experiential component and tend to expect God to reveal His will for their lives in fairly specific detail. In short, the Catholic in the Sword of the Spirit or People of Praise is a loyal member of the Church, highly motivated to serve God, demanding of his faith and its leaders. He believes that the Holy Spirit has led him into this community.

Earlier we mentioned the post-Vatican II upheaval of the late 1960s and how this shaped the context of the early charismatic renewal. During the early days of covenant communities (that is, during the early to mid-1970s), the Church seemed to be reeling from the changes of the 1960s. We knew that Our Lord wanted more of us than merely attending Mass once a week and confession once in a blue moon. The ideal of total self-gift and submission to God's will seemed impossible within normal Church structures. Covenant community, with its demands offered a chance for Christian heroism.

As a youngster in Catholic schools, I heard and was inspired by the lives of various saints. Then in 1974 I read a history of the early Jesuits. The courage, love and wholehearted commitment of Ignatius, Francis Xavier and the others again inspired a desire to give it all for Christ. But how could I, a married man with a child, live the kind of Christian commitment that Ignatius did? Not long after, Paul DeCelles came to my office and invited me to enter into "full-life submission" to Kevin Ranaghan, to become responsible for the pastoral care of others and to take up my position in the mission that the Holy Spirit was giving the People of Praise. Like many other men who had entered the People of Praise, I joined and committed myself more deeply to a call to serve. We all saw this as part of our service to the Church. We gave the community the devotion that the Church seemed unable to receive. By substituting its own inner dynamics and principles—namely the various aspects of its tangible grace, which correspond to the graces mediated through the Church—the covenant community supplants the Church in the life of the member. To be sure, the Church may very well have left itself vulnerable in certain ways—for example, by not effectively fostering a sense of communion within the parish community or by failing to challenge the apostolic potential of the laity. There is an experiential dimension to the life of faith that needs to be fostered and enriched. Certainly the communal character of the Church, especially at the local level, ought to be more than an article of faith, and so it is right to foster community. Nevertheless, the truth is that the diocese is the local Christian community and the parish is its neighborhood expression. This means that, as Pope John Paul II has insisted, any effort to develop Christian communities must be firmly rooted in the diocese.[115] Unfortunately, many Catholics have experienced the truth that most pastors do not really know what to do with parishioners who want to serve Christ more fully. I know: I have served on parish councils. However the experience in the community—especially strong in the first two years—of unity, of the "love of the brethren," of firm clear direction, of confident authority, and of mission tends to be strongly self-validating. "It must be real," and there is nothing like it in the "institutional Church." The covenant community is experienced as more real than the actual community. Thus it supplants the Church in the lives of its members.

Understanding this enables us to answer two very puzzling questions: (i) Why are unhappy members reluctant to leave? and (ii) Why are leaders so often devious and secretive?

(i) "Why don't unhappy members simply leave?" For someone outside a covenant community, this makes perfect sense. If they take 5% to 13% of your gross income and tell you how to raise your children; if you and your wife fight constantly about money and 'headship'; if you're unhappy and feel spiritually dead, why you stay makes little sense. Indeed, it is almost incomprehensible, even to priests and bishops, why members of these groups believe themselves so tightly bound in conscience.

The fundamental answer is that the loyalty or fidelity that Catholics typically have toward the Church is extended or even transferred to the covenant community. It is well known that most Catholics who leave the Church do so with a "bad conscience." The ex-Methodist used to attend a Methodist church, but the ex-Catholic is conscious of having "fallen away." Similarly, the covenant community member operates from a deeply ingrained presupposition that he or she is falling away or "letting down the Lord and the brothers and sisters."

Whoever enters a covenant community does so in an explicitly religious setting, after prayer and "seeking the Lord." Of course, their guidance in this comes from within the community. The presuppositions for decision-making are drawn almost exclusively from the charismatic experience.[116] Members are not encouraged to consult with people outside the community. The experience is one of a Spirit-led spiritual journey among the most Spirit-filled people. Therefore, to leave is to turn away from something that—so it seems—the Holy Spirit himself has done. Indeed, we recall that both People of Praise and Sword of the Spirit speak of entry into community as a response to God's will through the Holy Spirit.

Besides the conviction that the Holy Spirit has called one to this community life, there is the further conviction that its leaders are men anointed and raised up by God. From the very inception of the Catholic charismatic renewal, the juxtaposition of charismatic and institutional authority as two kinds of genuine spiritual authority has gone unchallenged. That is, few have questioned whether charismatic authority is authority at all. For the community member, these are leaders genuinely endowed with the gifts of being apostles, pastors, teachers, prophets, and evangelists. This conviction is reinforced by the recognition these men receive as charismatic renewal leaders, conference speakers, writers for *New Covenant*, diocesan liaisons, and the like. Photographs of leaders from both community systems alongside Cardinal Suenens and the Pope have been published in the Catholic and the charismatic press. Kevin Ranaghan was one of two liaisons for the charismatic renewal in his home diocese. These are leaders whom God has purportedly raised up. To follow them is a high calling, an honor, and an obligation. To oppose them is to oppose one whom Christ has raised up, and to leave without their permission is to be unsubmissive and rebellious toward God—indeed, to be disobedient.

Most decisive is that to leave the covenant community means leaving the most real experience of Christian community one has ever known. Worse still, it means separating oneself from the body of Christ. This is why people who leave these communities are often shunned by other members[117] and are spoken of as no longer brothers and sisters in Christ—or even no longer Christian. To be sure, the leaders of these groups will deny that there is a policy of shunning as such. What happens is that the person who leaves the community, or even seriously questions it, is recognized as "having problems". Out of charity and an effort to avoid negative talk, coordinators and other leaders do not discuss what these problems may be. It suffices that persons who ask be advised simply that "there are problems". To leave what one has experienced as the body of Christ entails either a complete rethinking of what that body is or an admission of spiritual failure with a consequent acceptance of guilt.

In short, leaving a covenant community is emotionally and intellectually far more difficult than changing colleges or careers or breaking a wedding engagement. It is more akin to divorce. The departing member knows that he is leaving not just an organization but an entire way of life. His or her weekly schedule is largely structured by required community events—men's or women's meetings, community service, the regular Sunday meeting, regular meeting with one's head. Life in community really is a *way of life*. Having invested himself totally in this life, he faces losing it all—and with it the most powerful and all-encompassing experiences of religion he may ever have had.

(ii). The deviousness and secretiveness of leaders. One of the more disturbing facts about these covenant communities is that the leadership consistently fails to be straightforward in its relationship to Church authority. The best-known instance of this arose from the pastoral visitation conducted by Most Rev. Albert Ottenweller of Steubenville. For several years, Bishop Ottenweller had approved the Servants of Christ the King, a Sword of the Spirit community, as a non-territorial parish. Responding to complaints by some members, he investigated the community and eventually insisted that it disassociate itself from Sword of the Spirit and undertake several specific reforms. One of his biggest complaints was that the leaders—whom he had trusted—regularly and systematically misled him concerning several key issues.[118] A particularly serious instance for the bishop was his discovery that there were two sets of financial records, an "official" set for the community as a parish (for the bishop's eyes) and the real records for the community leaders (to be withheld from Bishop Ottenweller). Indeed, throughout the investigation, the community leadership consistently "stonewalled" the process through scheduling conflicts, changed meetings times, protracted negotiations concerning conditions of dialogue, etc. The bishop was treated more like an enemy than a pastor. Likewise, when Archbishops Gerety and McCarrick of Newark ordered the People of Hope to sever their ties with Sword of the Spirit, the communities complied on paper but retained their structures and continued to welcome Sword of the Spirit leaders for teaching visits.

> In this context, a decision by the Sword of the Spirit Council is especially revealing.
>
> Some member groups, while sharing in collaboration with the SOS, may find it most helpful to engage in outreach activities and relationships with other groups under the title of Christ the King Association rather than Sword of the Spirit. Their collaboration with the Sword of the Spirit, while continuing fully, will not always be expressed publicly.[119]

This is nothing other than a decision to treat the Christ the King Association as a front group for Sword of the Spirit.[120] In other words, a bishop or priest concerned about an apparently

Catholic group may be unaware that he is actually dealing with an international ecumenical organization with a highly developed body of teaching and its own hierarchy.

We can cite an instance from the People of Praise as well. In late 1984, Pope John Paul II criticized the tendency of many "basic communities" (*communidades de base*) to separate themselves from local parishes and assume a life of their own. He stressed the importance of maintaining the parish as the center of Catholics' spiritual life.[121] His remarks were widely quoted in the Catholic press. In response, Paul DeCelles sent a note to all the coordinators of the People of Praise observing that the Pope had "balanced" his remarks by acknowledging that parishes cannot do everything. DeCelles added that the "basic communities" in question were Marxist groups predominantly in Latin America. Shortly thereafter, the People of Praise dropped the word "basic" from its covenant. In fact, most "basic communities" were not Marxist, and in any case, this was not the point of the Holy Father's remarks. As a result, the applicability of John Paul II's remarks to DeCelles' own People of Praise was completely blunted.

It would be tempting to say that such behavior is the exception rather than the rule, or that unfortunately some liars have gained positions of influence. However, without ruling out that some community leaders may dissemble consciously and deliberately, we must recognize that the false ecclesial claims of the communities are the principal cause of devious, secretive, and mistrustful behavior toward the Church. At the 1976 Theological Conference on the Catholic Charismatic Renewal, Fr. John Haughey, S.J. remarked that true leaders must find strength in their human weakness. In response, Word of God (now Sword of the Spirit) coordinator Bruce Yocum said that as covenant community leaders, they were the weakest of all, for they knew that all their work and planning could be undone overnight simply by a bishop's decree. More is at stake here simply than pride in and attachment to one's big life project. These men understand themselves to have created a new people for God. They see themselves as guardians and leaders of something that God, by a sovereign act of His will, has established. Indeed, they are the shepherds and guardians of Christ's flock. The use of the term "shepherd" has been very common in the history of these communities. Therefore, it is their responsibility before the Lord and on behalf of the flock to protect the community from every "attack," however well-intentioned and from whatever source.

In addition, we should note the effects of a false demonology that seems prevalent within the charismatic renewal. According to this understanding, the devil is able to use and manipulate the good acts of people in the state of grace to attain his ends. Thus, one who is obedient to God's eternal Word (and is thus in a state of sanctifying grace) may unwittingly oppose God's "now" word (and thus thwart God's plan).[122] This can play into Satan's hands. As a general rule, Satan opposes God and disrupts what God is doing. Therefore, if God is restoring unity to a divided Christianity and simultaneously establishing a bulwark against evil—achieving both ends by means of covenant communities—then anything that undermines these communities serves the devil's ends. Since the devil is constantly at war with God's people, and since his previous successes are especially threatened by the communities, he is evidently at war with the communities. Whatever works against the communities—even a bishop who believes he is exercising his rightful authority—is being used by Satan.[123]

In light of these considerations, it would clearly be the task of the leaders to protect what the Lord is doing. This often means concealing many details and allowing misconceptions to remain since Church officials simply do not understand how God is using the community. (Presumably, if they did understand, they would support the community.) Likewise, the directions that Church officials establish for the rest of the Church—as with the Holy Father's frequent statements on parish life—are considered not to apply to this unique and vitally important work that God is doing to build communities. Thus it is that good men can be led into deceiving and misleading even their bishop, regarding him as the unwitting tool of Satan.

Before concluding this section on false ecclesial claims and the covenant, we should consider the overall effect these have on the member's faith life. Typically, the first year or two in community is a heady, satisfying time, marked by emotional consolations as one's sacrifices of time and money are praised as signs of growth in the Holy Spirit. Many changes are occurring, new things are being learned, and one has a sense of growing. For many members, it is a time of bringing real order and peace to chaotic parts of their lives. Fathers take more concern for their children. Husbands and wives learn to communicate more clearly by making explicit agreements and asking forgiveness when they have done wrong. The "underway" member feels he must be on the right track. Inevitably, however, times of dryness come, and with them a testing of one's faith and love. It is perhaps here that the lie constituted by the ecclesial claims of the covenant community becomes most clear.

Ordinarily when the soul enters a time of dryness, the Holy Spirit is more deeply at work in it, transforming it in faith, hope and love. Deprived of sensible consolations, one is called to walk more by faith. If we understand that God is Spirit—indeed, that God is completely other and beyond any finite comprehension that we might have and beyond any human experience—then we see that such dryness must come. The disparity between human nature and the divine demands that the core of God's work in the soul be beyond experience. It is only reasonable that the soul experience times of dryness and difficulty, lest it identify God with sensuous experiences.[124] The time of dryness, then, is a time to approach God in faith alone, allowing him to work invisibly and imperceptibly in the soul through prayer and especially the sacraments. As it passes through such a time, even though it may never recapture the warmth of its earlier consolations, the soul comes to a conviction and confidence in God's love and to a certain sweetness and joy in suffering that are far better than anything that has gone before. Thus, a sound Catholic spirituality leads through dryness and suffering to joy; a spirituality focused on the Eucharist finds joy precisely in suffering.

The covenant community, however, provides no solution to the problem of dryness. Rather, it gives only this answer: Enter more fully into the life of the community. In practical terms, this means to be more faithful to one's community services, attending all gatherings faithfully, drawing closer to one's brothers or sisters (depending on one's sex) and submitting more fully and openly to one's head. In other words, the dryness is considered the member's own fault. A very common complaint of former members is that they had lived for years with a gnawing sense of being spiritual failures. A rather shy and withdrawn sort of person—in a high school play, although I had my lines memorized, I had no "stage presence"—I was passed over for any leadership role in the community. My personal head explained, "It's not the coordinators who have rejected you. God has rejected you." Subsequently, another head urged me to become more extroverted. Reflecting on my life in community, as well as in the Army and later in the world of work, I realized that I am, in fact, not a dynamic natural leader. But I was successful in the classroom, which is personally rewarding and, I trust, helpful to the students. God had given me many gifts, but not the gifts that community leaders valued. Leaders' exhortations to "jump in with both feet" and to "draw closer" are the most common counsels for spiritual dryness. Along the same lines, community retreats in the People of Praise are not so much opportunities to go off alone in silence to seek the Lord as occasions for reinforcing and expanding upon community teachings. The goal is not interior growth so much greater integration into the community.

The point of this critique is that by its very nature, the covenant community can reach only the social and psychological levels of the person, not the spiritual. Lacking both an understanding and the actual means of grace, the covenant community fails to meet the real spiritual needs of its members. The result is that after about two years, members typically begin sensing a growing spiritual dryness and drudgery with a consequent loss of joy.

CHAPTER 5.
PASTORAL CARE

Both Sword of the Spirit and People of Praise consider the pastoral care of their members integral to their communities. In both community systems, this is administered through a pyramidal structure of pastoral caregivers. Each member is assigned such a pastoral caregiver, to whom he or she is submitted. Originally both communities called these "heads," but in recent years, Sword of the Spirit has adopted the term "pastoral leaders" (or "governor" in *Patterns of Christian Community*). Every community member has one. For a married woman, her husband is always her head. However, realizing that a husband may well fail to be a satisfactory head for his wife, the communities supplement the headship of the husbands with the institution of *handmaids*, who are intended to be drawn from among the "wiser" women in the community. In the People of Praise, these were almost invariably the wives of leaders. For single women, this head is assigned by the coordinators, sometimes in consultation with the one being headed. Both community systems insist that their pastoral care is very beneficial.

a. Sword of the Spirit

The Constitution of the Sword of the Spirit defines pastoral care as "what the leaders of the Sword of the Spirit do to help members and groups to live the Christian life well."[125] This is illuminated by the community's statement of purpose:

> The primary purpose of our pastoral approach is to build up our members in living the Christian way of life. This includes belief in the fundamental Christian truths (the gospel, the creed). ... Central to the Christian life are love of God and neighbor as disciples of Jesus Christ. Such a life includes the keeping of the moral law, living it out daily in all our relationships. It also includes growth in Christian character, in faith, and in the use of the gifts of the Holy Spirit given to everyone for the building up of the body of Christ.[126]

Consistent with the vision presented in *Building Christian Communities*, Sword of the Spirit conceives pastoral care as the way by which the community makes people better Christians, by which it forms them.

Simply to understand Stephen Clark's vision of the Christian community is to grasp the essence of pastoral care in the Sword of the Spirit. We recall that the community is to be "one person," and that person is Christ. It is the primary means of Christian formation of its members, and it is the primary locus of holiness and apostolic activity. Shortly after the Word of God broke away from Sword of the Spirit, coordinator Bruce Yocum stressed precisely this point in an address to the Washtenaw County (Michigan) Community of Sword of the Spirit. Because of the split in the community, many members were left without pastoral leaders, and for a time the local coordinators had to sort through everything before assigning new pastoral leaders. The question arose as to how pastoral care would be managed or when it would resume. Yocum's response was that personal pastoral leadership is only part of pastoral care and, indeed, not the most important part. He explained that the coordinators care for the pastoral needs of the community through the life they teach and govern, through their guidance of the community as a whole. Such an approach is perfectly consistent with the vision Clark has of Christian community, and this understanding of the community as a collective person that forms its members is essential for understanding pastoral care in Sword of the Spirit.

There is a second vision—a metaphor—that appears in Clark's writings and which is very helpful for understanding life in Sword of the Spirit. It is the image of a traditional village society governed by tradition and the wisdom of its elders. In such a society the elders oversee the life of the whole, seeing to it that young men learn trades and young women learn the domestic arts and that their youthful unruliness is restrained, that family life runs well and irresponsible parents are called to account, and generally that everyone knows and takes up his place and relates well with the others. Under the wise and watchful guidance of the elder all the village needs are met, disputes are resolved, and the village lives in peace. It is a life characterized by well-defined roles, a maximum of interdependence and little concern for personal independence.[127]

From this vision of community and its supporting metaphor, it is clear that personal freedom and independence are discouraged in Clark's teaching. And indeed, Clark has specifically written:

> Many in the world hold up the ideal of independence of judgment and diversity of viewpoint, but in so doing they betray the fact that they are committed to individualism and not to genuine community. ... They (i.e., Christians) therefore, place a lower value on developing an individuality of approach or a more correct opinion than they do on coming to a oneness of understanding with the Christian community they are a part of.[128]

Read in the context of Frank Sinatra's "I Did It My Way" or of Madonna's outrageous and provocative antics, this position seems reasonable. Applied to mature Christians, it amounts to a denial of the right to individual personality. To develop one's own point of view different from others *even with an eye to forming a more correct opinion* is said to betray an individualism contrary to Christian community and inconsistent with the Christian life. One may better characterize it as a passion for the truth. Unfortunately, in the People of Praise we were often admonished that unity is more important than truth.

If personality were simply a matter of differences whimsically fostered for differences' sake, then to develop one's. individuality might well be unbecoming a Christian. The truth is, however, that personality is essentially rooted in the personhood of the individual human being. To be a person is to be an individual with a rational nature, which is to be endowed with intellect and will. By intellect we mean simply the ability to know and understand the truth, and by will we mean the power to love what is good and freely choose how we shall attain it. From the earliest days of Christian theology, the image of God in the human being has been found in the rational soul whose powers those are.[129] And indeed, God's command to rule over the earth and subdue it presupposes preeminently those powers of intellect and will, for only the knowing and understanding, loving and choosing being can be a true vicegerent for the Lord. Only such a creature can "tend the garden" and exercise dominion over creation.

The significance of this for our present discussion is that the human person is creative.[130] To possess the truth as one's own and personally to love the good and strive for it make one creative. This creativity is intended by God as part of our dignity. It is, of course, most visibly manifest in the work of cultural giants—Mozart, Shakespeare, Einstein—but any good teacher, caring parent, or diligent craftsman is likewise creative. True creativity flows not from self-centeredness but rather directly from a personal grasp of the truth shared out of a love for others.

We might further add that the Church has throughout her history been vitally enriched by the creativity of her saints. Consider: St. Benedict, who founded western monasticism; St. Francis and St. Dominic, who founded the mendicant orders; St. Catherine of Siena, who insisted the Pope return to Rome from Avignon; St. Teresa of Jesus, who reformed her order even in the face of episcopal opposition; St. Thomas More, who wrote *Utopia* and then later refused to follow almost all England's bishops into schism; Mother Teresa of Calcutta, who founded a new order to serve the poorest of the poor one at a time; St. Thomas Aquinas, who integrated Christian doctrine with the best of this world's wisdom.

It may, perhaps, seem that we read too much into Clark's critique of independence, but the remainder of his writings make clear that the community has absolute primacy. Within the Sword of the Spirit system it is virtually impossible that the members surpass their leaders or the community as a whole in holiness. All the criteria for goodness and truth are found in the community and not in the individual. More precisely, these criteria are found in the leadership of the community. Consider this remarkable claim: "If the elders do not love one another and are not one, the other brothers and sisters will not love one another and be one."[131] First of all, this is demonstrably false from experience. While we can readily grant that church leaders certainly should set an example of love and holy unity, no responsible authority teaches that the laity can love one another only as much as their priests and bishops love each other. More important, Clark makes the unity of the Church depend on the subjective disposition of its leaders and not on the objective work of Christ. Nevertheless it is consistent with and sheds a remarkable light on Clark's understanding of Christian community.

The community member is absolutely subject to the authority of the community. "Those who belong to a Christian community are subject to its authority for their whole lives. ... The government of the community therefore extends to everything in their lives."[132] This authority forms the basis for pastoral care. We must notice the phrase "for their whole lives." Although the Sword of the Spirit covenant allows for the possibility that one may eventually leave for good reason, the covenant is a whole-life event. In principle, it extends not only over the length of one's life—for even the decision to leave must be made according to the covenant—but also over the breadth and the depth, that is, over all the activities and the fundamental values or goals of one's life. To be sure, this authority is not so exercised in actual practice (as it would be—say—in military basic training) that all one's decisions are made from above. Nevertheless, many decisions are submitted to one's pastoral leader, especially those concerning career, marriage, and similar major matters. And the pastoral leader is free to broach any area of the life of the person he is pastoring.

Obviously such a system will not tend to foster one's growth in personal autonomy, self-definition or power. Indeed we have already noted that Sword of the Spirit rejects the emphasis on independence of thought and action, self-realization and self-fulfillment, and personal autonomy. The community is primary. The job of the pastoral leader then is to lead the member more and more into unity with the community, into submission to its leaders and to help with practical decision-making.

We need to look closely at this area of practical decisions, since it is fraught with significance for the Sword of the Spirit's understanding of God, the community, and the human person. Normally when wise parents guide their children in decision-making, they do so with an eye to the young person's growth in maturity and ability to decide for himself. Especially during the child's teenage years, the parents gradually "loosen the reins," proceeding from commands and prohibitions through permission to limited options to advice. The objective is that at the end of his adolescence the son or daughter will be on his own, able to make his decision freely, responsibly and well. And even though the parents may well stand ready to give advice to their grown children, they ought to do so only when invited, recognizing that their children are free to act otherwise. As they guide their children, wise parents normally have two goals in mind. First, they want the best or wisest decision made, at least in important matters. They forbid certain disastrous decisions and require certain essential ones (e.g., "You must take a foreign language in high school"). But second, they want their child to be able to choose for himself, and so they encourage him to do this (e.g., "You may choose French or German"). For a human person, the very act of freely making a decision and implementing it is itself a genuine value.[133] When they neglect this second goal, family problems result and their children typically rebel. And of course it is not always easy to balance these two goals. By way of contrast, however, in the Sword of the Spirit there is only one good and that is that the proper decision be made. Thus one must always have direction for life's decisions.

In the charismatic renewal in general and also in the covenant communities we find a serious confusion between God's will and God's choice. Indeed, precisely this confusion, this reduction of "God's will" to "God's choice," is the underlying, unspoken premise of Stephen Clark's *Knowing God's Will.*[134] God's will must always be done. Whoever does not obey God's will sins and hinders His plan. Now God's will in the most general form is given in the two Great Commandments: "You shall love the Lord your God with all your heart and with all your soul and with all your mind and with all your strength, and you shall love your neighbor as yourself." (Luke 10:27) These two commandments in fact are rooted in God's eternal will for all creation, that all things return to Him for His glory. As rational creatures we are destined for God in a special way, namely, to share His glory in perfect love, which will be eternal happiness. This is God's will, and He wills that we love Him and love our neighbor so that this eternal goal may be realized in us. But this is not the same as God's "choice." His will is that we love Him freely and that we devote ourselves freely to the authentic good of our neighbors. His "choice" is a problematic concept that can bind our conscience. Let us clarify what we mean.

It is fairly common in the charismatic renewal as well as in other contexts for people to experience "leadings of the Spirit." A classic (for charismatics) example is David Wilkerson's trip to New York to preach the Gospel to some young hoodlums who had just been arrested for murder. The result of this response of his to a spiritual sense he had was his very successful apostolate among the gangs in Manhattan. The almost impulsive response to what he saw on TV in his office changed Wilkerson's life and ministry for the better.[135] Likewise, in prayer groups across the country, Catholics have responded to "leadings of the Spirit," often with amazing results. One can easily conclude that God always or usually has very specific things He wants us to do and that, if we will but pay attention to signs, leadings, and prophecies, we can know what these are.

The false belief is this: that it is not sufficient to do God's will by loving Him and our fellow man, by becoming saints, but that God has some very specific plans for us involving concrete choices which He wants us to make; that God's focus has moved from making us into free agents of His love to making us slaves in His enterprise or soldiers in His army. The basis of this belief can be 1) a belief that God is doing something so new and different in this time that specific instructions are necessary if His will is to be accomplished, or 2) God is looking for specially dedicated and spiritually obedient servants who are willing to go beyond the "ordinary" Christian life to be perfect servants of God's will.[136] Or there may be a conviction that this is really the way God wants all men to live, but that only a few have the faith and the understanding to do it. In any case, what matters is no longer what I choose but what God has chosen.

One of the key points of Clark's *Knowing God's Will* is that the counsel of the Christian community's elders is an especially valuable source of guidance for finding what God wants. Clark discusses a variety of ways that the Christian may discern God's will, ways that are typically "charismatic" for the most part. However the Christian does not live in a vacuum, but rather he lives as a member of a body. For this reason, the leaders of that body play a prominent role in discerning God's will.

Now it is important to notice the implications of this. If the choice to be made is God's specific will, then not to do it is a very serious matter. In considering precisely this matter, St. Thomas Aquinas notes that to behave contrary to God's will would be mortal sin.[137] The reason is that God's will is not only the highest good for us, but it is also the standard for all other goods. To cut oneself off from God's will by turning away from it is to reject the fundamental principle of good. It is to choose against God.

Charismatics in general and community leaders in particular have not pursued the issue this far. Rather they tend to attribute to God an attitude that says, "If you will not do what I want, then I will find someone else who will obey My directions." A prophecy at the 1976 Conference of Communities, sponsored by the People of Praise and the Word of God expressed it thus: those present could turn down the invitation to join the bulwark the Lord was forming and still be saved, but they would be "left behind" and have much to endure in the coming trials.

In this highly charged spiritual context, the role of the pastoral leader is vital. "Submission to human beings is something God works through to form His people in His own likeness, to train them in submission to Himself, and to protect them from self-delusion and the deception of evil spirits."[138] Not only does the pastoral leader lead one to God's will, but he protects him from self-delusion and evil spirits. We must note here the immense capacity this system offers for manipulation.

To illustrate this more clearly, we cite two texts from Stephen B. Clark's *Knowing God's Will.*

> I believe that the Lord wants each one of us to know what he wants for us **at every moment**. He wants us to be his people, without doubts, without confusion.
>
> Our lives can only be formed by the Spirit when he guides us and we follow him. **Unless he shows us what we must do, we cannot live in the Spirit**. (emphasis added)[139]

The issue here is very starkly put. Confusion and doubts should not be normal experiences while making one's way through life. They are a result of not following the Lord. If one does what he wants, without knowing that it is specifically what God wants now, he is not living "in the Spirit." And so every natural factor in a situation—from one's desires to his abilities to his prospects—may point one way, but nevertheless, it is held that God may want something else for him, possibly something that had not entered his own head or heart to desire. The Christian winds up being totally dependent on whoever can know God's will with certainty. One friend of mine who held a good job in technology administration at the University of Notre Dame was offered a very good position, one that paid better than the University, at a local firm. He was strongly advised by his "head" to pass up this opportunity and remain at Notre Dame. Connections with the University were valued by the People of Praise. My friend, who had a young and growing family, took the new job against his head's counsel and left the community within a year. In the new job, he prospered financially and professionally.

In this example and in the theology of God's will as His choice that underlies it, we find an acute division between the natural and the supernatural. God's will, which is to be obeyed, is revealed only through community leaders, even if every natural factor in the situation points away from it. If the pastoral leader is to protect the member from self-delusion and the deception of evil spirits, and if God's will can be radically different from one's natural inclinations and gifts, then the individual community member has no inner resources of his own on which he can depend.[140] His wish to pursue something other than what the leaders propose may be self-delusion, rebellion, the deception of evil spirits or a genuine impulse for God. However, without the ratification of community leaders, he has no way of knowing whether God approves of his choice. As if to drive the point home, *Patterns of Christian Community* insists further: "Members of the community approach the elders as men who represent a body that the Lord has called together, and who therefore speak for the body and command the same commitment and honor as the body itself."[141] And when these elders give personal direction there is no higher court of appeals. To appeal outside the community is disloyal and brings discredit on the Lord's work.[142]

It is in light of this approach to pastoral guidance that we must understand published charges of "arranged marriages" in Sword of the Spirit.[143] Certainly this does not refer to a practice whereby two fathers work out an agreement and then inform their children that they will soon be married. Rather, pastoral leaders, under the direction of community elders, foster certain relationships and forbid others. Indeed they may very well insist that two single people of their choosing move towards marriage. Now, of all one's life decisions, the choice of a spouse and the decision to marry him or her *is* tied to deeply rooted human emotions and physical desires. Here especially one who wants to do only what God wants can be easily led to mistrust his or her own judgment. It is well said that love is blind, and in community the elders offer clear spiritual "eyes." As a result, good young people—ready to die to self and eager to please God first—can be pressured and manipulated into marriages not of their own choosing.

b. The People of Praise

As with the matter of ecclesial claims and covenant, the People of Praise understanding of headship or pastoral care is less starkly and clearly drawn than it is in Sword of the Spirit. Indeed some People of Praise documents speak impressively in places of human freedom, the richness of culture and the inherent dignity of the human person. Similarly, in the People of Praise we do not find the strong identification of the community with Christ himself, such as we find in Sword of the Spirit and therefore the impact upon one's conscience is not necessarily so strong. Nevertheless, much about the People of Praise pastoral system is flawed and leads to abuse. We need to examine it carefully.

The first thing to notice is that it is a pastoral system and intends to provide the Lord's pastoral care for its members. That is, pastoral care in the People of Praise is intended to enable the members to grow in righteousness and holiness and to judge and order their earthly lives with an eye towards their eternal heavenly goal.[144] It is intended effectively to replace the Church's established system of pastoral care. As noted earlier, members are discouraged from seeking the spiritual counsel of priests. When one goes to Confession, he should recite his sins, receive absolution, and leave. A remarkable example of the community's mistrust of the ordained pastors of the Church appears in a letter from senior coordinator Dan DeCelles to a community member who is also a professional counselor. The latter had questioned Paul DeCelles teaching in *Vine and Branches* on pastoral care. In the article Paul DeCelles had criticized counseling as being bound to the "here and now," without an eternal perspective. Dan DeCelles response to the counselor concluded with this remarkable paragraph:

> Perhaps an example would help clarify the problem Paul's describing. Someone goes to a Catholic priest for confession. He tells the priest what he's done and

> asks for absolution. The priest can see that the person feels guilty for his sins and tries to help the person feel better. Instead of helping him repent, the priest tries to build his self-esteem. He may succeed in the "here and now"; the person may go away feeling better about himself. But from an "eternal" perspective he may have caused some real damage.[145]

Besides the obvious fact that the penitent would not even be in the confessional had he not repented of the sins (at least out of "imperfect contrition"), one is struck by DeCelles' disregard for the effect of the sacrament itself, namely that the sins confessed are truly forgiven. The priest's words of counsel may be more to the point or less, depending on his own wisdom, inspiration, preparation, etc. (although DeCelles is in no position to judge). However, the eternal value of the confession derives precisely from the fact that this is the forum in which Christ chooses to forgive sin. In the confessional the priest stands in exactly the place of the good shepherd who goes out to seek the lost sheep and return it to the fold.

According to *Vine and Branches*, August 1992, the People of Praise has approached the Ordinaries of the dioceses in which its two largest branches are located and invited them to be involved in some way in the community's pastoral care. Both bishops declined, saying that they wish to pastor Catholic members through the parishes and other diocesan institutions. The significance of this is that the People of Praise sees itself as standing parallel, as it were, to these bishops and not under them. Therefore, it has apparently not even occurred to DeCelles and the rest of the People of Praise leadership that they might be bound to eliminate their own pastoral system and send their people back to the priests in the parishes. That is, People of Praise clearly understands itself to have a pastoral authority and ministry that is independent of that of the bishops of the Catholic Church. In that same *Vine and Branches* article, DeCelles justifies their independence by pointing to the lay character of the community and by noting that the borderlines between laity and clergy are not nearly so clear as they once were. Thus the member of the People of Praise is to understand that the pastoral care that he is to receive in order to grow in his life in Christ can only come from the headship of the People of Praise.

We should note the related point, that People of Praise steadfastly resists the notion that any churchman, including a bishop, has the authority to release a member from his obligation under the People of Praise covenant.

As the People of Praise claims to exercise an authentic pastoral ministry, it makes it effective and universal (within the People of Praise) by assigning a personal head to each member, except married women, who are pastored or "headed" by their husbands. We have already remarked that this is the practice common to People of Praise and Sword of the Spirit. "Headship" was also employed at the Episcopalian Church of the Redeemer in Houston, and it was picked up, either from the Church of the Redeemer or from the Catholic Charismatic communities by the Shepherding movement that was centered around the Christian Growth Ministries—Derek Prince, Don Basham, Charles Simpson, Bob Mumford and others.

While the People of Praise has attempted to distance itself from the shepherding movement in recent years, Paul DeCelles, Kevin Ranaghan, Stephen Clark, and Ralph Martin all worked very closely with these "brothers" from the shepherding movement. Three of the four founders of the People of Praise and the Sword of the Spirit were among the principal speakers at the 1975 National Men's Shepherds Conference in Kansas City, along with Christian Growth Ministries leaders. All the heads in the People of Praise were required to attend this event. Until late in 1980, Martin, Clark, DeCelles, Ranaghan and three of the Christian Growth Ministries pastors constituted a group called the Council, which met regularly to support each other in their ministries. Indeed, in 1975 this group made a secret covenant among themselves to support each other as "shepherds" and to bring about the unity of God's people. Thus the People of Praise pastoral system finds its roots and fundamental structure in the shepherding system which was adopted in different ways by several different groups. It is a mandatory system of headship organized pyramidically in such a way that every member is submitted to a head. Paul DeCelles has given teachings on "Discipleship" within the community teaching series, and the practice of "full-life submission" was for many years one of the cornerstones of the People of Praise approach to formation.

Two features of the People of Praise pastoral system are particularly problematic: 1) lack of confidentiality, and 2) confusion of governance with spiritual care. Concerning the first point: Although the People of Praise has a very clear teaching on "right speech," which forbids gossip and negative talk in general, heads are exempt from this when meeting among themselves. They typically discuss the problems of those under them so that the other brothers and especially their head can advise them how to handle the member's problem. What this means, of course, is that one can be reasonably sure that any information he gives his head about his own problems or weaknesses will go up the chain to the leadership. Furthermore, no one in the community may ask for or offer confidentiality in the headship relationship, for this would be to create an area of "darkness," cut off from the light of the Lord. Concerning the second point: The personal head is, on the one hand, a personal counselor and advisor, a guide who is to lead the community member into ordering his life in such a way that he achieves righteousness and holiness here on earth and attain to his eternal reward.[146] As such he is encouraged to pray for and take a strong personal concern for those under him.[147] On the other hand, the head is also the administrative link between the coordinators and the member. As such he is responsible for seeing to it that the member is faithful to his community responsibilities, such as meetings and his four hours of service per week, and communicating community policy and news. A specific responsibility he has is to determine from the member's gross income what his community support payment should be (at the very least 5% of the gross), and he should make sure this is paid.[148] Thus one's most intimate spiritual confidant is also the most immediate governmental authority.

These two aspects of People of Praise headship are a matter of grave concern and must surely give us pause. Taken together they imply that the People of Praise member's life is not his own, his or her self is not his or her own. As in Sword of the Spirit, the distinction between the secular and the religious is broken down, so that all one's decisions and dealings become the concern of one's head, and in turn potentially become known to the leadership. "It is the capital sin of pride not to reveal all your thoughts and opinions to your head for correction," taught Sharon Rose, a community handmaid or leader of women, at a women's retreat. "Not to be open with your head concerning your budget is a manifestation of the sin of greed," according to Joseph Heintzelman, a branch head. (Both teachings were given with the express approval of the head coordinators.) Everything that a member does is in principle subject to the review and judgment of the coordinators. Furthermore, the progress of his soul falls directly under their rule. The effect is almost necessarily that the good of this soul will be the implementation of the goals of the community leaders, for the interpreter of God's will is also the messenger and administrator for the coordinators.[149] If the community member feels himself or herself called by God in a direction for which the People of Praise provides no context or in a direction somehow contrary to what the community is doing, he is strictly "on his own" spiritually. His head will normally oppose him, and he is pressured at least to be absolutely sure that God wants something else of him. Furthermore there is a strong temptation not to be completely forthright with one's head, since whatever one says may indeed go "up the tubes" to community leaders.

In the later years of our membership in the People of Praise, when Marie (my wife) was increasingly at odds with the community leadership and its structures and I was not, she decided it would be best for her to try harder to belong. Happy to accommodate her submissive wishes, my own head assigned her to meet with a handmaid.[150] At her first meeting, this woman told her that the project was to peel her "like an onion" of all her previous views and opinions and then to build her back up as a community woman. She was to have no will or identity of her own. In particular, if I, as her husband (and therefore head) should accuse her of some wrongdoing, she must—even if innocent—repent and ask for forgiveness. The handmaid's plan failed miserably in this case. Marie's distrust of community leadership was definitively confirmed. It should be noted that this handmaid, like others in the community, had no training in theology nor psychology.

It is instructive to contrast this with the Church's practice. The confidentiality of the confessional is primary here. Any Catholic may confess any sin, no matter how heinous or how often committed, and his confessor is absolutely forbidden to take it with him out of the confessional, not even to his bishop or the pope, much less to another priest or lay person. This seal of confession extends even to persons who might act as interpreters or translators in the confessional or who even simply overhear.[151] Furthermore, the Church resolutely seeks to prevent governmental considerations from interfering with the care of souls in such a way that the latter is compromised. Thus, recognizing that most seminarians will be eager for ordination, the Church forbids that either the candidate's confessor or his spiritual director have any say concerning his admission to ordination.[152] The Church will risk ordaining an unsuitable candidate to the priesthood rather than to compromise anyone's access to the forgiving mercy of God. By contrast, at a meeting in 1985, shortly before my dismissal from the community, my own head advised me that everything we talked about was strictly confidential. Subsequently, my comments to him were cited as reasons for my dismissal from my job at Charismatic Renewal Services.

In recent years People of Praise has taken belated steps to provide training for those who are to serve as heads. This training is based largely on Pope St. Gregory the Great's *Pastoral Care*. In and of itself it is good to learn from the Doctors and saints. It must be kept in mind, however, that Pope Gregory wrote his work as a handbook for the bishop, to aid him in the pulpit. He did not envision that lay leaders of an extra-ecclesial group would assign lay pastors and require weekly meetings for pastoral counselling, as the People of Praise does. Even if the content of their pastoral counsel is drawn from impeccable Catholic sources, it remains true that the shepherding-discipleship structure is not Catholic and that this very structure determines what impact pastoral care will have.

The section on "Authority" in *Spirit and Purpose* is very enlightening. It begins with the statement, "All authentic authority is generated by Jesus Christ as head of his body, the church." By the next paragraph we read, "Yet there are some gifts which are designed for the overall health of the whole body, and those who are given these gifts accept the burdens which come from major responsibilities." Here we see that the reference has shifted from the Church to the community. The remainder of the section proceeds to cite the relevant Scripture texts, including Hebrews 13:17: "Obey your leaders and submit to them; for they are keeping watch over your souls, as men who will have to give account." The clear implication of the section—which carefully avoids stating this directly—is that the "pastors" of the People of Praise enjoy the authority Christ has given to his Church and that the members of the community are bound to submit to them. This is, in fact, how the members of that community understand their relationship with their leaders.

Nevertheless, these heads are not really pastors. Most of them are not ordained nor are they subject to the oversight, whether direct or indirect, of the local bishop. Therefore, they cannot effectively minister Christ's saving love to those under them. Neither are they educated in the Church's rich teachings on spiritual direction. They are restricted to merely human means such as teaching, exhorting, persuading, scolding and ridicule. They simply do not have the power to administer the means Christ has provided to effect an inner transformation of the soul. Thus, the People of Praise pastoral head cannot confidently entrust the soul to the Lord, leaving him or her in peace to respond freely to the Lord's interior workings. Rather the head must constantly prod, question, urge and exhort, using these visible means to produce visible result. Indeed, Paul DeCelles has gone so far as to endorse the use of ridicule and scorn to lead others on into Christian commitment.[153]

For several years, I too served as personal head for some men in the People of Praise. After my dismissal from the People of Praise, I approached one of them, Jim, to ask if I needed to ask his forgiveness for anything I might have done while serving as his head. He responded, "Not really ... except for this. Like every other head I had, you seemed focused on what was wrong with me, on my 'problems'." Unfortunately, Jim's comment was very much on the mark. Even as we claimed to form a bulwark for Christianity, we regarded our own selves as weak, crippled by our problems.

It is worthwhile to cite the words of Fr. Henri de Lubac, who insists that the true pastor enjoys a "paternal" authority, which derives directly from the fact that the priest is ordained to act in the person of Christ. That is, the priest is "father" precisely in virtue of the sacramental character of his priesthood. De Lubac writes that if this paternal authority be suppressed,

> either it would be necessary to renounce all spiritual authority and preach anarchy, or the Christian would be unavoidably subjected to an authority that was abusive in its very principle, and consequently tyrannical, however benign its forms and conditions of use were originally conceived to be.[154]

The manipulative approaches recommended by DeCelles are precisely the behaviors that have given rise to reported abuses of power within these communities. Lacking the means of grace, these pastors must resort to the manipulation of souls and consciences.

One final aspect of pastoral care in the People of Praise needs to be noted here, and that is the community's practice of deliverance from evil spirits. The community's *Pastoral Guidelines state:*

> Normally within the first year of being underway each member of the community is prayed with for deliverance. Normally this is done in a general deliverance session.
>
> It is also normal for people to be prayed with again for deliverance if they and their head feel it would be beneficial for them. (Lk. 10:19-20)"[155]

Overall coordinator Paul DeCelles once remarked that prior to the "discovery" of deliverance from evil spirits, it had been impossible to form community. Kevin Ranaghan commented in August 1977 that without deliverance, "We would have been just a happy little Holy Spirit group." This prayer to expel oppressive spirits was therefore a gift of the Lord to make possible the common life of the People of Praise.

The theological conception underlying this prayer is that most (if not all) Christians can be consistently "oppressed" by certain evil spirits—such as a spirit of confusion or lust or deceit. Unlike cases of possession, in which the subject's body is actually taken over by an evil spirit, this oppression consists in a particular spirit's "hanging around" his victim to impel or incline him almost constantly in the direction of a certain kind of sin. On the basis of this distinction, the community further distinguishes between exorcism (which is required in the case of possession) and deliverance from oppressing spirits. As such, the prayer allegedly does not fall under the canonical requirement that exorcism be performed only by a priest with "the special and express permission of the Ordinary."[156] Nevertheless, the Congregation for the Doctrine of the Faith in 1984 expressed concern over laypeople using prayers ...

> "in the course of which the demons are directly disturbed and attempt is made to determine their identity. This applies even to cases which, although they do not involve true diabolical possession, manifest diabolical influence."[157]

The manner of this prayer is for the prayer leaders and the subjects of deliverance to pray in common for a period and then to break into teams which pray with individuals one at a time.

> Then individuals are prayed with by a smaller team which includes the person's head. When a woman is being prayed with at least one woman should be on the team. The team does not "interrogate the spirits," but rather discerns their presence and prays against them in the name of the Father, the Son and the Holy Spirit. The person being prayed with is to renounce any spirits that are named.[158]

The method here is significant. We note that, except for

offering up his own prayer, the one prayed with is passive. The evil spirits that are oppressing him are discerned by others, and he is simply to renounce them. So, a member of the prayer team may say, "I sense a spirit of greed." In sacramental confession the subject always accuses himself and has the right and freedom to deny any sin or area of sin which the confessor priest may ask him about. In deliverance, the discernment is done entirely by the prayer team; there is no discussion, debate or dialogue. If the team discerns—say—a spirit of rebellion, one is not to examine his conscience or behavior to discern whether this is true, but he is simply to renounce the spirit. In subsequent meetings with his head, he will be guided into practical steps for living out that deliverance and growing in submission. The practice also leaves the door open for manipulation by leaders. For example, in the deliverance prayer over someone who has asked hard or critical questions about the community or its leadership, a "critical spirit" or a "spirit of rebellion" may be "discerned." By the very nature of the situation, this is not an accusation against the person being prayed with. He is simply the "victim" of evil spirits. A protestation or denial on his part would be to no avail; indeed, it would be considered as not "yielding" to the grace of the prayer. From that point on, the subject of the prayer knows that with every criticism, he is playing into the devil's hands. If he forgets, his pastoral head will be able to remind him that, by the very act of criticizing, he is falling into Satan's plan for his life, to lead him away from God. It should be noted that with sacramental confession, the priest is bound never to refer to what has been confessed to him. So, if Max has confessed to the abuse of alcohol to Father Louie, and the next day, the priest sees Max leaving a bar, unsteady on his feet, he *absolutely may not* mention Max's confession from the day before.

A further point is in order here. Also unlike sacramental confession, there is no seal of confidentiality. Although prayer teams are urged not to gossip about what goes on in the deliverance session, it remains 'pastorally' appropriate to discuss the results of the prayer with others in headship within the community so that the coordinators can better take concern for the subject's pastoral needs. It is also the case that if one should admit to an area of sinful inclination—say, strong homosexual temptations—then that information can and ordinarily will be communicated to others in authority within the community.

The abuse and potential manipulation of consciences constituted by the practice of deliverance is one of the most serious defects of the People of Praise. The community's perspective on spiritual warfare, with its concomitant belief that as the People of Praise it is competent to discern and expel evil spirits from the lives of its members, is a key reason that members feel spiritually threatened by the prospect of leaving the community.

c. Summary

Pastoral care within both Sword of the Spirit and People of Praise is gravely defective in principle. The basis of it is a false belief that there are charismatic gifts of the Holy Spirit that qualify one as a pastor of souls, combined with a false confidence that these communities are full Christian communities, that is, local manifestations of the body of Christ. But these beliefs are unwarranted. Neither Sword of the Spirit nor People of Praise nor any other such community has any ground for assuming that God has entrusted it with the care of souls. The Church throughout history, up through the Second Vatican Council and the pontificate of John Paul II as expressed very clearly in *Pastores dabo vobis*[159], has insisted that Christ has entrusted his pastoral mission only to the Apostles, their successors and the ordained coworkers. In them and only in them does the One Shepherd exercise his ministry. For another to claim this office is not only presumptive, but it is also false and a usurpation of Christ's authority. It is well to keep in mind Christ's ominous words regarding such shepherds.[160]

These pastoral systems are not harmless. Growing evidence, along with a proper understanding of their dynamics, suggests that these systems cripple community members psychologically, reducing them to fear and bondage rather than liberating them for the authentic freedom of sons and daughters of God. We have already established how the covenant community supplants the Church. Under the People of Praise or Sword of the Spirit pastoral system, one's primary spiritual reference point is his head. If he is the pastor Christ has given me, then I am best assured of pleasing Christ by following my head or pastoral leader. The teaching of the communities repeatedly reinforces this point, and coordinators frequently exhort members to bring problems or questions to their heads. Likewise, one never hears guidelines for testing or discerning the advice of one's pastoral leader, except for allowing appeals to his head's superior. The teaching and practice of "right speech" result in the fact that most community members speak positively of their relationship with their pastoral leader. Headship is always praised, never criticized in public. The effect, of course, is that the member who has misgivings or doubts is very much alone. What everyone else speaks so highly of must be good. Any problem is with the doubting member. And this doubt is itself a serious defect in commitment.

We need to take especial note that both systems, Sword of the Spirit and People of Praise, effectively close the door to pastoral help from the Church. Stephen Clark's *Patterns of Christian Community* calls it "disloyalty," a grave offense, to take one's problems and disagreements to someone outside the community.[161] The People of Praise, as mentioned, discourages its members from seeking the counsel of a priest. Thus the member is left with only the perspective that what Christ has for him and what Christ wants of him can be found only in the community.

It is impossible to regard the pastoral systems of Sword of the Spirit and People of Praise and to find them healthy, either in theory or in practice. Both are destructive and should be treated as such.

CHAPTER 6.
ECUMENISM

Both Sword of the Spirit and People of Praise regard themselves as ecumenical communities, although individual local groups within Sword of the Spirit may be Catholic. In virtue of this ecumenism those communities claim to offer a distinctive hope and opportunity for the Christian people, and they claim exemption from certain strictures that would normally apply, were they exclusively and explicitly Catholic organizations.

On the face of it, the underlying ecumenical theory that these communities assume seems logical. It runs roughly as follows:

1. As Christians we share in common something far greater than that which divides us, namely our faith in Christ. Likewise, what divides Christians from the world is much greater than what divides them from each other.
2. By our faith we are made brothers and sisters in Christ, co-heirs with him of the Kingdom.
3. Christ commands us to love one another by laying down our lives for each other as he did for us.
4. Therefore, Christians should be able to share the great wealth of faith that they have in common and live in

> relationships of committed servant-love, regardless of differences between their churches.

The communities' approach is to accept a fundamental doctrinal core[162] of Christian truth and then lead all the members into a life of practical committed love for one another. In this way the communities are founded on faith in Christ and love of the brothers. The Bible is the norm for teaching, especially those books accepted by Protestants as well as Catholics, and since community teaching is predominantly practical rather than doctrinal or theological, there should be little risk of falling into heterodoxy or heresy.

The apparent beauty of this approach is that it requires no doctrinal or denominational decision. Every member is free to embrace the teachings and practices of his own denomination. As a community, then, they express the common core of faith and live out exemplary lives of love. What is required for this to work is a kind of courtesy called "ecumenical sensitivity," and both community systems have guidelines for this.

In Sword of the Spirit, as could be expected, the guidelines are spelled out clearly and in fair detail. The guiding principle is that in public or official manifestation of the community life, distinctly denominational symbols, beliefs, and practices should not be given prominence or any special authority.[163] So, if a teacher cites the book of Wisdom,[164] he should support it with a text from Proverbs. It is acceptable to cite Aquinas occasionally, provided one also refers (for example) to Calvin or Luther. Religious art that is specific to one particular denomination (e.g., crucifixes and statues of Our Lady) should not be used in public areas, including community offices and public areas of community homes such as living and dining rooms. The crucifix belongs in the bedroom or private den. Public prayer will avoid denominational manifestations—such as the Sign of the Cross and the Hail Mary. (The "for Thine is the Kingdom" is normally appended to the Our Father, even though Catholics hardly ever use it).

The Sword of the Spirit's rules for interpreting of Scripture are particularly significant. The Sword of the Spirit constitution refers to doctrinal divisions and the corresponding diverse interpretation of Scripture as the product of polemics between various groups. The teacher in Sword of the Spirit, then, who is dealing with a controverted text should find a spiritual meaning, a sense that can address all denominations and not support the claims of one over against another. So, for instance, "we should stress the *authority* of Scripture as the word of God rather than its all-sufficiency, or its insufficiency without tradition or the church Magisterium."[165] What the Church itself teaches, however, is something different.

> *But the task of authentically interpreting the word of God, whether written or handed on, has been entrusted exclusively to the living teaching office of the Church, whose authority is exercised in the name of Jesus Christ.*[166]

The People of Praise is less specific than Sword of the Spirit, although its practices are similar. Particularly noteworthy is the treatment of ecumenism in *Spirit and Purpose*. There it is stated:

> We realize that our communion will grow as our churches themselves achieve a proper form of unity.... However, the highest expression of Christian unity remains a distant summit which our Lord desires for his disciples.[167]

In the meantime, People of Praise will share among themselves the unity that is possible for them "as our churches permit." It is, on the face of it, a modest and reasonable approach to ecumenism.

The overall guideline within the People of Praise is

"Ecumenical sensitivity," and its manifestations are similar to those mandated by Sword of the Spirit. Members are encouraged to express themselves with ecumenical sensitivity at all public functions of the community. And conscious of its predominant Catholic majority, the community takes pains not to look "too Catholic." When Kevin Ranaghan spoke briefly at the 1984 Worldwide Retreat for Priests in Vatican City, the editor of the People of Praise's magazine *New Heaven/New Earth* took great pains to avoid illustrating the story with photographs of the Pope or St. Peter's Basilica, as these were too distinctively Catholic.

In many contexts such an approach of "ecumenical sensitivity" makes sense. One thinks, for instance, of the interdenominational effort to protect the unborn. It would be pointless to insist that everyone in an Operation Rescue effort go to Mass first or that a Right to Life demonstration be led by a priest. When Christians gather to accomplish works of mercy, they can ignore their differences for the sake of the work at hand. Furthermore, Christians of different denominations can share their daily lives in peace, harmony and love. Really, that is the basis for a Christian civil society. However, neither People of Praise nor Sword of the Spirit claims to exist for limited charitable goals, and neither claims to be a civil society. They claim to be authentic Christian communities, and it is here that this "ecumenism" becomes problematic.

The ecumenical approaches of Sword of the Spirit and People of Praise are based on a fundamental misunderstanding of what the Church is. Both systems of communities have adopted the *de facto* stance of observers "above the fray" and outside the Churches. Clearly, if we take the Sword of the Spirit guidelines at face value, the member's denominational affiliation is a private matter. He is not present in the Sword of the Spirit *as a Catholic*, since his Catholic identity is relegated to the private sphere. The central ecclesial fact of his life is that he belongs to a Sword of the Spirit community. In a more subtle, but just as real way this same dynamic is at work in the People of Praise. The entire community lives in as much unity as possible in the hope of someday attaining the "distant summit" of full unity. But the truth is that all the Catholic members of the People of Praise are joined in a full, deep, and wonderful unity with the Lord and with each other when they celebrate the Eucharist and receive communion. The Church *is* one. The unity granted by Christ in the Catholic Church is ignored in favor of a unity that People of Praise hopes to enjoy when denominational unity might be established. On this we may consider what the Second Vatican Council has to say.

> This is the one Church of Christ which in the Creed is professed as one, holy, catholic, and apostolic, which our Savior, after his resurrection, commissioned Peter to shepherd (John 21:17) ... This Church constituted and organized in the world as a society, subsists in the Catholic Church, which is governed by the successor of Peter and by the bishops in communion with him, although many elements of sanctification and of truth are found outside of its visible structure.[168]

Sword of the Spirit and the People of Praise misunderstand what the Church is, and this is most especially clear in the "ecumenically sensitive" down-playing of certain specifically Catholic manifestations of faith. For example, both systems avoid public references to and veneration of the Blessed Virgin Mary as something offensive to Protestants. But the ecclesiological significance of Mary is essential: She is the Mother and Model of the Church.[169] Not to acknowledge her is not to know the Church as mother. This is no mere metaphor here, either. The economy of the Incarnation is that just as Mary was indispensable for bringing Christ to birth in the world, so is the Church—the institutional Catholic Church—necessary for the world to encounter Christ. And indeed, if we neglect the motherhood of Mary then we will surely overlook the living maternity of the Church and, in fact, see it as only an institution. Mary is integral to the faith, not an extraneous or non-essential object of sentimental devotion.

The Church is most fully herself when she celebrates the Eucharist. With their emphasis on covenant commitment and the experience of community, People of Praise and Sword of the Spirit make the Body of Christ (i.e., the authentic Christian community) extrinsic to the Church, which is reduced to the role of a service institution. This form of ecumenism, which attempts to live a corporate life of faith independent of any one church and outside the context of the Eucharist, is a merely human venture. Wherever Mass is celebrated, Christ is saving His people by offering up a perfect sacrifice to His Father and by laying down His life for them. He is gathering them into one.

> For by Christ's will there is in this sacrament a continual renewing of the mystery of the sacrifice of himself that Christ offered to the Father on the altar of the cross, a sacrifice that the Father accepted ...[170]

It is sheer arrogance to claim to establish greater unity by a covenant among men than that which Christ has established and is establishing by His own blood. If these groups are genuinely concerned for the unity of Christ's people, they will lead them not into covenant but to the Eucharist.

Here we must mention one of the most curious and, indeed, aberrant manifestations of the ecumenism practiced by the Sword of the Spirit and the People of Praise. In the summer of 1975, Stephen Clark and Ralph Martin (The Word of God), Paul DeCelles and Kevin Ranaghan (People of Praise), Don Basham, Ern Baxter, Bob Mumford, Derek Prince and Charles Simpson (Christian Growth Ministries), Larry Christenson, and Don Pfotenhauer (Lutheran charismatics) made a covenant among themselves "to care for and serve what God is doing to restore and reunite his people."[171] This Council, consisting of four Catholics, two Lutherans and five non-denominational ministers constituted the motivating and ideological force behind the 1975 National Men's Shepherds Conference in Kansas City and the 1977 Conference on Charismatic Renewal in the Christian Churches.

The latter event, which took place in Kansas City, Missouri, was the showcase of the People of Praise and The Word of God's ecumenical approach. Every morning the various denominational renewal groups (such as the Catholic National Service Committee) held their sessions in smaller facilities around town. Then in the evenings all 50,000 participants (of whom 46% were Catholic) met for the general sessions in Arrowhead Stadium. After the conference the Council concluded, "God has given us a mandate to become *one*. Kansas City (i.e., the 1977 conference) was a forerunner of a greater unity. The unity of the Kansas City Conference grew out of *our* unity."[172] The members of the Council spoke of themselves as "imparting unity" to the body of Christ from their own unity. At this point in its existence, the Council saw as its mission the establishing an interdenominational network of communities covenanted to one another, their leaders being trained as disciples of the Council.

Among the various specific projects discussed in 1977 was a Leadership Training Institute for young men to be sent into ministry. This institute would be staffed by three teachers, "each from a different tradition" (i.e., Catholic, Protestant, non-denominational). Such an institute would "affect the spiritual and academic leadership of the Church ... train and equip teachers for the Body of Christ," in the expectation that "such training would provide protection for the Body of Christ."[173] Cardinal Leon Joseph Suenens had earlier proposed a training institute for men to be ordained into the Catholic priesthood and diaconate. The Council proposed founding this Leadership Training Institute in response to and (they apparently hoped) with the blessing of the Cardinal. The minutes conclude: "We work *with* Cardinal Suenens, but *our* communities would be in charge."[174] The minutes of this meeting, amount to an unabashed discussion of how to use a prelate who had gone to great lengths to foster the charismatic renewal in the Catholic Church and ensure its recognition by the Holy See. Interestingly, Cardinal Suenens was one of the Council Fathers of the Second Vatican Council, having played a significant role in its deliberations. He volunteered to work with the Catholic charismatic renewal leaders to guide them in realizing the spiritual renewal called for by Vatican II and promised by the charismatic movement.

As it turned out, the Council passed out of existence when the People of Praise parted company with The Word of God in 1981. The Protestant members of the Council offered to mediate the dispute between Clark and Martin on one hand and DeCelles and Ranaghan on the other. The People of Praise coordinators declined, however, observing that since the four principals were Catholics, the mediation should be by a Catholic authority.

With the dissolution of the Council, the great plan for imparting unity through a tightly committed network of interdenominational communities failed. Instead The Word of God turned to the formation of the Sword of the Spirit network, while the People of Praise formed an association of communities, which was eventually transformed into the present form of the People of Praise. What remains significant about this episode is the ecclesiology and ecumenical understanding that underlay this project. The various churches, including the Catholic Church, were regarded as institutions that may embody traditions, but which were incapable of realizing true unity on their own. The unity Christ wants for his people was to exist only in explicit, covenantal relationships. The Body of Christ was to be something existing outside of and—indeed—"over" the Catholic Church. The unity of God's people was not something inhering in the Catholic Church but rather was to be imparted by a group of unordained men—most of them not Catholic—who stand in a covenant relationship with each other.

The Council's vision of imparted unity may have died in 1981, but the communities' practical ecumenism persisted. Yet this is not sound either. First of all, the practical, denominationally independent approach to interpreting the Scripture is deceptively simplistic and dangerous. A recent essay by Archbishop Antonio Ambrosiano of Spoleto Norcia (Italy) explicitly rejects such an approach:

> Ecumenical 'initiatives and activities' should not be understood in a restrictive sense such as could evoke a kind of pragmatic ecumenism made up of things and activities that prescind from doctrinal principles and from the professions of faith themselves. On the contrary we call 'ecumenism' that which begins with activities and initiatives undertaken to foster the dialogue of truth by confronting doctrinal issues and deepening our understanding of them in view of a common faith.[175]

In fact, the community approach could be much more accurately called "non-denominational" rather than "ecumenical."

In fact the Sword of the Spirit characterization of doctrine as merely the result of polemics borders on the heretical.[176] The Church is not only Mother but she is teacher as well. Her office of teaching is intrinsically related to Scripture. That is, Christ has bequeathed His Revelation to the Church, which is its guardian, and that Revelation is contained in a unified and privileged way in Sacred Scripture. The Scriptures belong to the Church as her book. To interpret them independently of the Church is immediately to begin to falsify them. We may say that the Church herself is the living interpretive key for understanding the Bible.

Furthermore it is the Church's express teaching that Christ gave His Apostles and their successors, the Bishops, the authority to teach authentic Christian doctrine.

> Sacred Tradition and Sacred Scripture make up a single sacred deposit of the Word of God, which is entrusted to the Church.... But the task of giving an authentic interpretation of the Word of God, whether in its written form or in the form of Tradition, has been entrusted to the living teaching office of the Church alone.[177]

While others may certainly read, reflect, do theology and comment on the Scriptures, the Catholic bishops under the Pope remain the authoritative teachers. To approach the Scriptures independently of them, for instance in some non-or trans-denominational way, is to reject precisely the means Christ has provided for understanding His Word. We cannot—out of "ecumenical sensitivity"—pretend that there is an interdenominational way to read Scripture faithfully.

Concerning the Scriptures we must also insist that even a non-dogmatic and practical approach to the Bible constitutes a falsification of it. If we say, as Stephen Clark does, that the Scriptures intend to teach us about social structures and roles, or if we present them as simply the life of Christ and the people of God, along with practical wisdom for following Christ, then we have reduced them to less than they really are. Indeed, if we read the Scriptures in the way proposed by Sword of the Spirit, People of Praise and their leaders, then the Church itself disappears from the Bible, and this is certainly not the mind of Christ.

Both Sword of the Spirit and People of Praise see themselves as making a vital contribution to the cause of Christian unity by providing a model and an example of living Christian unity in their communities. Yet it is hard to see the fruit of this initiative. After more than forty-five years of these communities, they have had no real impact on the ecumenical movements. We have not seen new initiatives, new dialogues, flourishing fruits. The hoped-for results have not yet appeared.

What is also troublesome about these communities taken as ecumenical initiatives is that they are not following the directives established by Vatican II for ecumenical activity. The Decree on Ecumenism, *Unitatis redintegratio*, is very clear about the basis of our unity in Christ. It is Christ's work of salvation, accomplished on the cross, and given to the Church.

> In his Church he instituted the wonderful sacrament of the Eucharist by which the unity of the Church is both signified and brought about. He gave his followers a new commandment to love one another, and promised the Spirit, their Advocate, who, as Lord and life-giver, should remain with them forever.

and further on,

> It is through the faithful preaching of the Gospel by the Apostles and their successors—the bishops with Peter's successor at their head—through their administering the sacraments, and through their governing in love, that Jesus Christ wishes his people to increase, under the action of the Holy Spirit; and he perfects its fellowship in unity; in the confession of one faith, in the common celebration of divine worship, and in the fraternal harmony of the family of God.[178]

These communities undertake an important project of common life and common prayer without any oversight from any bishop. The Second Vatican Council grants that occasional ecumenical prayer services may be of value, but these communities do much more than to meet for weekly prayer and fellowship. The Church insists that those who undertake ecumenical endeavors be well-grounded in Catholic teaching and that they proceed on the basis of that teaching. But members of Sword of the Spirit and People of Praise proceed on the basis of a nondenominational "community teaching."

The Church, in her maternal concern, has always jealously guarded the Catholic identity and consciousness of her children. Indeed, so far as ecumenical or interfaith communities are concerned, she has been historically reluctant to approve the founding of that most basic community, marriage, on an interfaith basis. The reason for this has nothing to do with ecclesial possessiveness. Rather the Church recognizes that she is the necessary and sufficient means for salvation and that to weaken a Catholic's allegiance to the Church is to imperil his salvation. As ecumenical ventures, Sword of the Spirit and People of Praise are unauthorized, misleading, and dangerous.[179]

To conclude this section, we must comment briefly on the claim sometimes advanced that because these communities are "ecumenical" and not Catholic, as such they are not subject to the authority of the local bishops involved. This simply is not true. First, since these groups have Catholic members (including the top leadership), those members fall under the direct spiritual authority of the bishop. In no way can membership in a covenant community be construed as removing one from that authority.[180] Secondly, if these communities are serious about their ecumenical commitment, then they must be answerable to the bishop, precisely because he is the one responsible for ecumenical outreach and mission in his diocese. In this as in too many other similar matters, we can let our social conventions and courtesies obscure the truth. In this case, the truth is that the bishop is responsible for *all* the souls in his diocese—for evangelizing those who do not believe, for leading the separated brethren back into unity, and for the care of practicing Catholics. The notion that the bishop has no jurisdiction over such a group—especially one whose members are predominantly Catholic—is simply false. To suggest otherwise is to betray a serious ignorance of the nature of the bishop's pastoral office and of the filial relationship a Catholic owes to him.

CHAPTER 7.
WOMEN, MEN, AND THE MARRIAGE RELATIONSHIP

The most visibly objectionable aspect of these covenant communities and those modeled after them is the set of practices regarding women, men,—the two sexes—and married life. While the doctrinal bases of these practices and even the teachings themselves may vary somewhat among communities, the practices themselves show a remarkable similarity.

In both the Sword of the Spirit communities and in the People of Praise, women play a decidedly secondary role to men. Indeed, it is hard to see what benefit women *as women* receive from membership in a covenant community. St. Paul's stipulations in 1 Corinthians 11 and in Ephesians 5 that the husband is the "head" of his wife and that the wife is to "submit in all things" are taken as a fundamental pattern for marriage. A married woman is expected always to reflect the fact that she is under her husband's authority. This goes beyond an acknowledgment that the husband is "head of the home" or head of the family; he is, in fact, her personal pastoral head. Whatever she does requires at least his tacit approval. He is responsible for her formation and growth in the Christian life. When my wife received some bad and possibly harmful direction from a handmaid,[181] the coordinator responsible for our branch of the People of Praise directed me to recognize that she was in fact resisting God's plan for her life. The fact that the handmaid's advice was bad was irrelevant. His advice did, however, have this positive result that it induced me seriously to consider my wife's evident spiritual maturity and spiritual independence from me, to recognize that although I may sometimes be helpful to her, I can also be misguided. In either case, she was answerable to God and not to me.

Women in general take a secondary role in the life of the community. Although women may prophesy at community gatherings, no woman may hold a position of leadership in which she governs men.[182] All leaders (coordinators) must be men. The communities plainly disapprove of women serving in leadership positions. When the People of Praise (South Bend branch) celebrated the "Festival of Lessons and Carols" in a Methodist church whose pastor was a woman, the pastor was not invited to read the Scripture text normally reserved for the host pastor. That same community's plan for mission in the Caribbean islands states: "We should probably deal with the Caribbean matriarchal system by quietly developing an alternate rather than encouraging a confrontation."[183]

Before examining the specific patterns of life and teaching of these two groups, it is worthwhile to consider the sources of this tradition. Although Catholics have written prolifically on the subject of marriage and the nature of the human being as male and female, precious little community teaching is drawn from these sources. There is no discussion at all of Mary as the exemplary woman. When Pope John Paul II issued his Apostolic Exhortation, *Familiaris consortio*, and his Apostolic Letter, *Mulieris dignitatem*, neither community system incorporated this teaching into their practices and teaching. Pope John Paul II's Theology of the Body[184], an almost revolutionary body of teaching on love, the human body, and marriage, which clarifies the deep truth behind the biblical teachings on sex and love, including the challenging texts from the writings of St Paul, was completely disregarded by the leadership of these covenant communities.

The teaching of these communities is drawn from and—indeed—taken over from fundamentalist Protestant sources. Stephen Clark (The Word of God/SOS) and Kevin Ranaghan were members of the planning board of the National Men's Shepherds Conference in August 1975, an event which many men in both communities were required to attend. This conference was co-sponsored by the independent pastors of Christian Growth Ministries and other Protestant leaders. We have already seen in the previous section how this group saw itself as the men on whom God was going to rebuild his people. An important aspect of this event was precisely that it was a *men's* shepherds conference. The teaching of such men as Bob Mumford and Charles Simpson on manliness, fathering sons, and the role of women was influential for these communities. These men as a group accepted as a fundamental principle that according to the divine order only men were to govern others. The basis for this was not sacramental but social; God has ordained that men shall lead. For women to lead men, especially in the Church, is an aberration. It is no surprise that all these communities see feminism as one of the principal ideological evils of our time.

a. The Sword of the Spirit

The more definitive and systematic teaching on the marriage and the roles of men and women is found in the Sword of the Spirit. Stephen Clark's *Man and Woman in Christ*[185] is a detailed exposition of precisely that teaching and a justification for it. It is not conceived "parochially" either, as though "this is just how we do it here." Clark fully intends his account in *Man and Woman* to lay out how God intends for all men and women to live.

Fundamental to Clark's position is that God has ordained a specific social structure according to which for human beings should live.

> The New Testament teaches more than matters of belief (what some would call 'doctrine') and universal ethical principles. It also teaches a social structure for those who have found faith in Christ and are being built in him into a new human race.[186]

Integral to this social structure are social roles, in particular the roles of men and women.[187] The paradigm for these social roles is the role of husband and wife in marriage.[188] And the pattern for husband and wife is a very sharply defined hierarchical relationship, in which the husband is the "head" of the wife. The wife is absolutely submitted to her husband.

The immediate basis for this pattern in marriage is the series of texts—mainly Pauline—in which wives are instructed to be submissive or subordinate (e.g., Eph. 5:22-33; 1 Cor. 11:2-16; 14:33-36; Col. 3: 18-19). A prominent theme running throughout the book is the authority of God's word. Clark devotes several sections to refuting contemporary forms of exegesis that evacuate God's word of its authority, so that Christians are not bound to obey it. Precisely this point is vital if we want to understand the effect of this teaching and the subsequent bondage that men and women fall into because of it. For the most part, members of covenant communities have come into them from their experience in the charismatic renewal movement. There they have experienced God as powerful and his word as something personally addressed to them. Having experienced the power of the Risen Lord, for instance, they have little patience with scholarly interpretations which seem to reduce the Resurrection of Christ to a "faith event." Furthermore, most of them have had, as a component of their conversion experience or "baptism in the Holy Spirit," a sense of being convicted of former sins and of repentance for them. They want to remain on the path of obedience to the Lord. Having effectively repented of sins that even priest may have excused (and here I am thinking of things like impure acts, fornication, homosexuality), they are suspicious of anyone who seems to propose that God no longer means what he said in Scripture about sin. The result of this is that within such communities, the presentation of Ephesians 5: 22-33 as God's command to be obeyed finds a receptive audience, even if the substance of the command is distasteful. It is better to die to self than to disobey God's word.[189]

Clark maintains that his conclusions flow from the sense of the Scriptures and that his interpretations of the texts in question are in the mainstream of Scripture scholarship. In fact, Clark insists that his approach to the Scriptures is neither innovative nor controversial. The controversies arise because of a "liberationist" bias in certain authors.[190] Nevertheless, he comes up with conclusions that are unparalleled in "mainstream" Christian theology and that conflict significantly with the understanding presented by the Church, a conflict that stands out starkly to the reader of Pope John Paul II's Apostolic Letter *Mulieris dignitatem*. It is instructive to compare Clark's approach with that of the Pope, and we shall address this comparison shortly. First, however, it is important to show the radical nature of Clark's understanding.

In most cultures and traditions, the husband has been regarded as head of the family and the home. In many cases this has even carried with it a certain supremacy and honor above all other members of the family or household. Father's word may be law, binding even upon his wife. He might well be "boss" and receive various privileges. Yet even in their most autocratic expressions of male authority, such cultural forms fall decisively short of Clark's conception. The husband as head of the home is analogous to a governmental figure. He governs the family as a unit. Of course, this may well mean that he exercises very direct and even autocratic authority over others in the family.[191]

Clark's conception of the husband's authority goes far beyond this, even if in everyday life the result may appear to be similar. Properly speaking, the husband's is the only personality in the family, for the family is "one person" and the husband-father is the head. Consider these texts:

> The husband and wife are to be 'one flesh' or '<u>one person</u>' with the husband as head.[192]

> The husband and wife are supposed to be one person; within that oneness the husband stands to the wife as the head to the body ... The two are supposed to function as one, and consequently the wife's life must be completely under the authority of her husband as head.[193]

Clark moves from the Biblical "one flesh" (Gen. 2:24) to "one person," and he takes this transition to be unproblematic. We may note that he never considers that there may be a need to justify substituting "person" for "flesh." His concern is to characterize the close unity that exists between husband and wife and, indeed, within the Christian community as a whole. In fact, the terminological shift is of critical importance. The term "person" was originally adopted to enable theologians to render an account of the Trinity. Even within the ineffable unity of the Godhead there subsists a real distinction of Persons.

A *person*, according to the classical definition of Boethius and accepted by Catholic theologians since, is the "individual substance of a rational nature."[194] If the married couple or the family as a whole is but one person and not the individual human beings within it, then for the part (i.e., the individual human being) to act on his or her own is to act irrationally and divisively, for it is the group which is properly "the individual substance of a rational nature." For one member to act "on his own" and not in submission is to break the unity of the group. We recall that Clark has said that the wife is to her husband as the body to the head. If together they are one person, then her lack of submission to the head is analogous to the twitching of a spastic person's arm. The wife is to do and to be precisely what her husband, as head, requires. As head, he is the principle of unity for the whole family.

It is vital to see that we are not splitting philosophical hairs here. Rather, Clark's "one person" theory of the marriage relationship reveals a great deal about his conception of unity among human beings and, *a fortiori*, among Christians. We have already remarked how, in his understanding of community, there is virtually no room for decisive disagreement or conflict with leaders. For Stephen B. Clark, unity means submission of mind and will to the one who is the head of that unity—in marriage, the husband. Here we might reflect on the relationship between Saints Bonaventure, a Franciscan and Thomas Aquinas, a Dominican, who were close friends in Paris in the 13th century. They also differed sharply on some important issues, such as the nature of angels and the faculty of the soul that possesses happiness. To this day, we find Franciscans insisting that their man is right and not the Dominican.[195] The two principals, however, remained good friends.

At this point it is worthwhile to look at an alternative view, that true union among human beings consists in loving communion. Addressing the question of the two wills in Christ (the human and the divine) Cardinal Ratzinger comments:

> With this interpretation of union as communion the (Third Council of Constantinople) sketches an ontology of freedom. The two 'wills' are united in the way in which two wills can be united, namely in the common affirmation of a shared value.[196]

Clark's conception is juridical and, indeed, administrative. His conception depends ultimately on a kind of decision-making model. Unity means working as a team, as a kind of social machine. For two individuals to be as one, that is, in unity, they must operate with one understanding and one will.

Otherwise, they will interfere with each other and not be in unity. For Clark, unity means doing things in the same way.[197] For the married couple to act as one, he believes, they can have but one will, and this is the will of the husband. Ratzinger points to a different kind of unity. Two human beings can enter into union not by submerging one within the other's will but by their sharing a common value, that is, a common love. This is the unity of friends.[198]

This distinction is all important. In Clark's conception, the person submitting stands in the relationship of a servant or a tool toward the other. She (or he) is to accomplish the will of the head. While intelligent "input" may be in order before a decision is made and a certain intelligence may be called for in the execution of that will, the recognition of the real truth of the matter at hand and the actual decision as to what should be done always belongs to the head. Thus a good wife, according to Clark's conception, is in a position analogous to that of a well-trained hunting or police dog, with this exception—that she can carry out more complex tasks, such as planning and preparing a six-course meal.[199] "She should be a loyal partner who he can count on as part of his own person."[200]

On the other hand, Cardinal Ratzinger's conception of unity as communion depends on precisely those factors by which the human being is a spiritual being, by which he or she is a person. The two spiritual faculties or powers of the soul are the intellect (or power to understand truth) and the will (or power to love and choose the good). A fully human act, therefore, is one which flows from the person's own understanding and choice of the good. To will means freely to choose one's own act on the basis of this knowledge and love. Only in such a way is one's act fully human and only in this way does it have true spiritual worth. The Second Vatican Council writes: "It is, however, only in freedom that man can turn himself towards what is good."[201] Two human beings are in true union, not when they do the same physical action, but when they love the same thing.

This same point has been virtually a hallmark of the thought of Pope John Paul II. In his *Love and Responsibility* he argues strenuously that one person may never be reduced simply to being a tool of another, for another's use. An essential characteristic of the person is his or her interiority or inner life, from which flows the power of self-determination or free will.[202] Ultimately it is the sharing of a common love that makes union—including the marital union[203]—possible. Far from creating a rigid hierarchy, such a union demands a fundamental equality between the two. "When two different people consciously choose a common aim this puts them on a footing of equality, and precludes the possibility that one of them might be subordinate to the other."[204] Clark's approach effectively negates this fundamental human equality between man and woman.

Equally significant is the emphasis in Clark's study on the functional aspect of human relationships and the complete neglect of the erotic. Indeed, the reader of *Man and Woman in Christ* finds that although the word "love" seldom appears, "effective" and "functional" (and their cognates) appear repeatedly throughout. The love that the husband is commanded (by St. Paul) to have for his wife amounts mainly to meeting her physical needs, rather than her emotional ones.[205] Now Clark contends that he presents the Scriptural view of the relationship between husband and wife. Yet the Scriptures clearly and favorably present the erotic as integral to human love. The Old Testament background to the famous passage at Ephesians 5 in which wives are told to be subject to their husbands and in which their relationship is compared to the love between Christ and his Church is the highly erotic Song of Songs, celebrating the physical love between man and wife as the model of God's love for his people.[206] Isaac desired Rebekah. Jacob loved Rachel. The wisdom literature encourages the husband to rejoice in the wife of his youth (Proverbs 5:18; Ecclesiastes 9:9) And of course, Adam was delighted when he first met Eve. Clark pays but scant attention to this aspect of love between man and woman. He presents this aspect of the marital relationship as something of a modern deviation, one of the unfortunate fruits of technological society. Indeed, his *Man and Woman in Christ* comes very close to defending "arranged" marriages; he specifically endorses that marriage be undertaken more for the good of the social group than for the satisfaction of the man and woman involved.[207]

We are not here facing simply a fact about human nature which Clark overlooks, but rather a point of profound theological importance. Stephen Clark consistently downplays the role of desire, emotion, yearning and love in the Christian life in favor of the decisive, the definite, the committed. The Sword of the Spirit "Community Weekend" series (given to prospective members) teaches that the basis of the Christian community is the covenant, understood as an agreement. In virtue of a *commitment* to each other, people become brothers and sisters; "when we make a covenant we relate to one another because we are committed to one another, not because of need or desire." The same is true of marriage, according to this talk.[208] Without a doubt, commitment is important to the Christian life. However, the basis for commitment is love. The primary reality is the human being's need of and longing for God. It is the erotic in relation to God, and it affects the very structure of our Christian lives.

This primacy of need and desire is abundantly clear in the writings of the great saints. One thinks of St. Francis de Sales *On the Love of God*, with its constant evocation of the sweetness of God's love, of the exquisite imagery found in John of the Cross' *Dark Night of the Soul*:

> One dark night, fired with love's urgent longings—aah, the sheer grace —
>
> I went out unseen, my house being now all stilled.

> [...]
>
> I abandoned and forgot myself; laying my face on my Beloved;
>
> All things ceased; I went out from myself, leaving my cares forgotten among the lilies.[209]

Perhaps the most famous and oft quoted reference to this yearning for God is from St. Augustine: "You have made us for yourself, and our heart is restless until it rests in you."[210] Less poetically but in detail with greater precision, St. Thomas Aquinas explains that all human action is inspired by the desire for the perfect good, which is found only in the vision of God.[211] Whatever commitment the Christian may make, it is preceded and accompanied by God's activity in drawing him to his own immense Beauty. The persistence in faith, hope and love which characterizes the life of a saint is a grace from God. Its origin is not in the personal commitment of the saint himself. We need to make commitments, but even more, we need the desire for God's love to maintain us in those commitments.

If this is true of one's relationship with Christ, so too does it hold in that intimate relationship between husband and wife. It is not insignificant that the strongest yearnings and the most intense pleasures and joys a human being can experience pertain precisely to the union between husband and wife. Indeed, it is that very pleasurable experience of making love physically, and not the verbal and mental commitment, which renders the love between the couple fruitful. By their satisfaction of that yearning for each other they become parents and thus share in the work of the Creator.[212]

These teachings have led to significant aberrations within the Sword of the Spirit. From its earliest days, the community regulated dating and courtship. The steps toward marriage have been a matter for direct involvement by community leaders.

> "Marty had gone to his pastoral leader to ask about me," Kathy says. "And then his pastoral leader had talked to my pastoral leader. My pastoral leader had given permission for me to enter into a dating relationship. But all this time, I had no idea any of it was going on." Only when Marty asked to see her again did Kathy realize that she was the target of a formal marriage suit.[213]

I have personally spoken with three women whose marriages were "arranged" by community leaders in the Sword of the Spirit. This typically happened when pastoral leaders setting up the dates (or encouraged them) and then rushed the persons concerned into engagement and marriage. In one case, the woman was actually required to repeat after her pastoral leader, "I do want to marry N.," when she expressed misgivings. Of these three, one marriage has ended, another is in grave trouble, and the third couple has left the community, while facing the fact that they never would have chosen each other on their own. They are successfully learning to love each other.

b. The People of Praise

The doctrine of the People of Praise concerning women's roles and of the marriage relationship is characteristically less developed than in the Sword of the Spirit. There is certainly no major work to compare with *Man and Woman in Christ*. Indeed, the leaders of the People of Praise have attempted to distance themselves from the teaching presented in Clark's book.[214] Nevertheless the patterns and the structures of life are remarkably similar to those of the Sword of the Spirit.

The foundational documents of the community offer little indication that a strong gender-role distinction plays an important part in the life of the community. *The Spirit and the Purpose* states: "Families retain their identities as natural units under the overall authority of the father."[215] This can be taken, of course, in a sense no stronger than that the father is head of the family. Another section, on "Outreach," states:

> Another aim of our apostolic action is to confirm the family in its vocation by establishing right order in its spirituality and relationships.[216]

This is followed immediately by the text of Ephesians 5: 21-27; 6:1,4. The version of this document with Catholic annotations lists St. John Chrysostom's *Homilies on the Epistle to the Ephesians*, 20, as a reference to this. In this text, Chrysostom stresses the role of husband as "head" and the wife as a second authority in submission to the husband. The reference to one of the great Church Fathers is unexceptionable, of course. However, it is significant that no mention is made here to Pope John Paul II's Theology of the Body[217] or his Apostolic Letter, *Mulieris Dignitatem*,[218] which differently interpret and sharply circumscribe the husband's headship.

Nevertheless, the People of Praise approach to women, as well as to marriage is badly skewed, and this has been formally expressed in other documents. In a memo on "Caribbean Outreach" from the early 1980s, the community's "Christians in Mission" outreach lists as one of its three objectives:

> "Strengthen Christianity in the Caribbean through fostering and training male leadership."

This is to be accomplished by gathering strong, promising men into "cell groups" and training them. The document further recommends:

> We should probably deal with the Caribbean matriarchal system by quietly developing an alternate rather than encouraging a confrontation. The strategy of small groups can probably accomplish that. It amounts

to planting some good seeds and hoping they will grow and not be squeezed out.

What is proposed here is not simply a strategy for an apostolate, but rather a reforming of an indigenous culture. If Christianity, as the People of Praise understands it, is to be planted in the Caribbean, then the (perceived) matriarchal system is an element that cannot be inculturated. A culture that accepts women in overall social leadership is to that extent incapable of being Christianized. For the People of Praise the subordinate role of women to men is a fundamental cultural premise. Of course, the father is the family's head and principal disciplinarian. The mother has authority of her own. She is more than simply the enforcer of father's commands. She has a particular concern for the formation of her daughters. According to a teaching that Dorothy Ranaghan gave the women of the People of Praise, they should strive to raise their daughters to imitate them as "carbon copies!".

Within the People of Praise, all men and women meet weekly in small, single-sex groups for sharing and formation. It is not deemed appropriate for them to meet in mixed groups for this. A man finds his primary relationships within his men's group and the woman finds hers within her women's group. The community's Trinity Schools (grades 6 through 12) also enforces fairly strict separation of the sexes.[219]

The most significant statement of the People of Praise position concerning women and marriage, however, is to be found in an interview with Paul DeCelles in Vine *and the Branches.*[220]

> V&B: How is pastoral care given to married women in the People of Praise?
>
> Paul: From their husbands normally. They also receive pastoral care from the coordinators, who are responsible for all the people in the community.

As "head" of his wife, the husband is her pastor. He is responsible to help her grow in her relationship with Christ and as a member of the community. He leads her in discerning God's will for her life. In the community's early teachings on the headship of the husband over his wife, Kevin Ranaghan suggested that the husband's care for his wife is salvific, that her salvation is in a certain way mediated by him as he lays down his life for her as her head in imitation of Christ's washing the Church by the shedding of his blood (*Eph.* 5: 25-27). We must add that this teaching, that the husband is spiritual head or pastor to his wife is one of the most firmly held and foundational teachings in that community. "Pastoral care primarily has to do with the husband assisting his wife in every possible way to grow in holiness and goodness before the Lord."[221] It is the ideal actively striven for in every home, extolled at community celebrations and discussed in weekly men's groups and women's groups. The significance of the headship relationship in the People of Praise can hardly be over-emphasized.

We may immediately draw attention to two serious problems with this practice. The first is that it subverts the basic equality that exists between husband and wife. Recall from the earlier discussion of pastoral care in the People of Praise that the head has a pastoral concern for every aspect of the life of the one headed. He is the one who ratifies whether initiatives are "from the Lord." He is the one who discerns God's will. He is the one who represents the coordinators to the one headed. Thus the wife, as a good member of the community, has a *prima facie* obligation to obey her husband as the bearer of God's will. In practice, this means that the two do not—indeed, cannot—relate as equals. His will reveals God's to her, whereas her will is merely human (if not even "of the flesh"). If she becomes angry and argues with him, then she may very well be charged with resisting God's will.[222] The two cannot meet as equals, because the husband always has divine authority on his side. As a matter of fact, in the People of Praise marital difficulties are most generally attributed either to the husband's weakness or the wife's rebellion. If she steadfastly refuses to accept community teaching and order—or especially if she does not want to belong—she will be described semi-publicly as "having emotional problems."

This first difficulty ties directly into the second one. As the equality of husband and wife is denied, their unity is subverted by the introduction of the husband's head as a third party. We find the warrant for this in the article by Paul DeCelles, cited above. "These pastors (i.e., the coordinators) are given spiritual gifts that enable them to help the husband's ordinary gift of heading the wife work better."[223] The husband needs to rely on the wisdom of his head and especially of the coordinators to lead his wife well. Although in principle the husband and wife ought to communicate, the weight of the wife's views is significantly different from that of his head's. This means that, in both theory and in practice, what husband and wife decide is subject to review and approval by the husband's head. The wife never has a say greater than the head's.[224] Therefore even within the intimacy of a marriage, the primary relationship is vertical, within the community hierarchy, rather than horizontal. Within the marital relationship there is always a third party, namely the community leadership (as represented by the husband's head). For husband and wife to try to work out difficulties and a mutual understanding on their own is considered wrong. DeCelles comments: "You can have a conspiracy of silence between husband and wife sometimes. It's a real tragedy."[225]

According to the People of Praise, for the husband (or any other head) to head well, he must be "transparent." That is, he must communicate what has been told him by his head or community leadership without changing it and without representing it as something he might not agree with. He must "take responsibility" for the teaching or policy by representing it as his own. So, if his head should say that the children need to go to camp, then the husband says, "*I* think the children should go to camp." The effect of this is that real dialogue between the husband and his wife is impossible, because he is no longer himself but the "mind-of-the-community." She never knows whether he is saying what *he* wants or what *they* want. Thus true dialogue between husband and wife is crippled, if not destroyed.

What John Paul II thinks

Almost simultaneously with the publication of Clark's *Man and Woman in Christ* in 1980, Pope John Paul II began delivering his Theology of the Body teaching.[226] Like Clark, the Pope begins with the creation narratives in Genesis and moved through the Scriptures to the New Testament and particularly to the Letter to the Ephesians, chapter 5. However, John Paul II's approach is fundamentally, radically different from Clark's. Instead of searching the Scriptures to find God's rules for conjugal relations, John Paul II looks first for God's intentions for human beings from the beginning. The first man, Adam,[227] was a *person*, that is, an intelligent being with intellect and will. When God presented the animals for him to name them, Adam could not find among them a suitable partner because he recognized his inherent superiority to them. *He alone* could think and decide. Unlike them, he had an inner life, a spiritual life. In virtue of this he became a partner of the Absolute. Then God cast him into a deep sleep and formed the woman. When he awoke, his response was, "This one at last is bone of my bone and flesh of my flesh!" The first man recognized that in her was a person like himself, one with whom he could relate personally and in truth. She too was a partner of the Absolute. As a person she was not there to meet his needs, like the horse that could pull his plow or the dog that could herd his sheep. Their relationship had to be different. We read that they could become one flesh and that in their one-flesh union they were not ashamed to be naked. (This was before the Fall, which spoiled almost everything.) Their relationship was not to be one of use or simply enjoyment. It was to be one of personal communion, a mutual total gift of self. Indeed, John Paul II remarks that the image of God was most fully realized in the union of the two. We must emphasize that for Pope Saint John Paul II, there is no question of inequality or subordination between man and woman. As persons they were made for each other.

In the early 1990s, as I was speaking to a group of former covenant community members about this fundamental equality of man and wife, one listener insistently asked, "But what about Ephesians 5?" He was referring to the verses,

> Wives be subject to your husbands, as to the Lord, for the husband is the head of the wife as Christ is the head of the church, his body, and is itself its Savior. As the church is subject to Christ, so let wives also be subject in everything to their husbands. (Ephesians 5:22-24)

For John Paul II, this is a key text. However, "if one wishes to *interpret this passage*, he must do so *in the light* of what *Christ* has told us about the human body."[228] He absolutely rejects the notion that this relationship authorizes any kind of dominion or rule of the husband over his wife. Rather,

> "He expresses a different concept instead, namely that it is her relationship with Christ [...] that the wife can and should find the motivation for her relationship with her husband, which flows from the very essence of marriage and the family. This relationship is nevertheless not one-sided submission. [...] The source of this reciprocal submission lies in Christian pietas and its expression is love.[229]

The 'rule' governing the relationship of husband and wife is the rule of love, which is the rule of mutual submission. This rule is founded ultimately on the analogy of the love relationships among the Persons of the Blessed Trinity.

Family and Misogyny in Communities

At first glance, the teaching and practices of these two covenant community systems might be nothing worse than the misapplication of some controverted passages of Scripture along with a very traditionalist view of the place of women. In fact, the problem is innate to the very structure of these groups, and it has to do in part with the loss of a Marian perspective. Given the preponderance of Catholics in both groups, amounting to about 95% in one, it is surprising to find that the Blessed Virgin Mary has no place in their life or spirituality. (We may recall that the four men who founded these groups were all affiliated with the University of Notre Dame du Lac, "Our Lady of the Lake.") This neglect of Our Lady is a spiritual defect with far-reaching and decisive consequences.

The Church itself is mother, and Mary is Mother and Model of the Church.[230] To understand Mary is to understand the Church and vice-versa.[231] In particular, Mary reveals the maternal character of the Church. Precisely this character has been lost by the covenant communities under consideration. The task of the mother is to nurture life by giving selflessly of herself. The mother bears a human being – she knows not whom – within her body for nine months. When the child is born, she first nourishes it from her own body and then by her hands. She is ordinarily the first teacher of language, of manual skills, and of human love. What she most clearly does not do is to manufacture her child by means of some technique. She is rather at the service of the unique life of her own child. Such is the maternity of Mary and only so can the maternity of the Church be understood.

Having neglected Mary, the communities have lost sight of what the Church, including the local Church in its communal manifestation, must be like. They have chosen instead a pastoral system under which members are formed by means of external forces and techniques, rather than one which fosters the life of faith within. They build, structure and manipulate according to their own principles, but they fail to nourish and nurture the person's own spiritual life that was imparted at Baptism. The communities may be rightly charged with being over-masculinized.

Complementing the teachings and practices governing masculinity was community doctrine on the family. Of course, the husband/father was head of the home. In *some* cases, heads sought to and even did exercise authority over the home life of those under them, even to the point of trying to direct men in their professional careers. Children were under the authority of their parents (both father and mother). Their religious training was left to the parents and their school or parish programs. In People of Praise, younger children were watched during community gatherings by the children's ministry. Their instruction consisted largely of Bible stories and songs. The important thing was that a child be raised to become a full member of the community. The coordinators taught that children ultimately belonged to the Community, as whose representatives the parents served. Strict, but not harsh, discipline was encouraged. "Tough love" was the disciplinary ideal, and its implementation was left to the discretion of the parents.

The most significant impact of the Community on family life was the existence of headship, especially the headship over the husband/father. He was encouraged to share about his family life with the other men in his men's group, of course. More important, however, were his regular meetings with his head. With him conjugal and family life were inevitably topics of conversation. Most heads expected those under them to disclose their household budget and submit it for evaluation. The relationship with one's wife and the discernment of her *real* needs (as opposed to those she expressed) fell under the head's authority. Although this headship could be intrusive, it generally was not significant. What *was* significant was that the husband's head was implanted invisibly in the home. Of course, wives were ordinarily sensitive to this, knowing that what went on at the dinner table or in the bedroom may well be a matter for the head to discern and discuss. All this was necessary for the life of the Community to go on in the home.

As a result, the contribution which women can make has been seriously undervalued in these organizations. Women are valued primarily for childcare, both for their own and for children of their sisters and for serving the men, to whom falls the primary responsibility for the group's apostolate. However, Pope John Paul II has written, "In God's eternal plan, woman is the one in whom the order of love in the created world of persons first takes root."[232] Indeed, he stresses that the father must learn his fatherhood precisely from his wife, for she is much closer to that role in virtue of having born and nursed the child.[233] If the woman is simply an extension of her husband's person (as in Clark's writings) or if her relationship with God is fundamentally mediated by her husband and subject to his authority (as in the People of Praise), then her unique and privileged perspective on the love of the human person will be obscured, if not lost. An immediate fruit of this is that a kind of wall is built up between men and women in general and between husband and wife in particular.

Men in Community

These covenant communities were, in a sense, made for men. The old blues lament, "it's a man's world," holds true in People of Praise and The Word of God/Sword of the Spirit. Community life did not make men's lives easier, although men were subtly discouraged from helping too much with household chores. The great value of community life for men is that it gives them a mission. In the community a man knows who he is. Indeed, we may say that he gets his identity from the community. He is one of "the brothers" who shares the important mission of the People of God in today's sinful world. To be singled out favorably by one of the coordinators is something of an honor. A man wants their approval, especially (for those in the People of Praise) the approval of Overall Coordinator Paul DeCelles. When men of the community gather in prayer, they believe they form a kind of bulwark against the evil in this world.

Covenant communities like People of Praise and The Word of God stressed manliness. It was a bad thing for a man to be "femmy." For them, feminism was a serious evil in our society, an evil that was subverting the Church. Feminism and its manifestations had to be resisted. God's men had to be soldiers, brothers fighting powers unseen. Steve Clark taught that one of the hallmarks of masculinity was the readiness to "crush the enemy." For a time, The Word of God required men to wear mantels to community meetings, as the women wore veils. In the People of Praise, men did manly things, even to the point of playing poker on retreats. Falling in love was a form of insanity. For a man to be controlled by his wife was a bad thing, and women at one point were exhorted in prophecy to "set these men free!" Manhood in the covenant community was about strength and purpose, a sense of belonging to a group of strong men. In marriage and family, the man was the head the head of his wife. He should not allow her to dominate him.

Both communities have developed a clear sense of "men's work" and "women's work."[234] A man who involved himself in women's concerns or who enjoyed the company of women too much was seen as being "feminized." The People of Praise even made it a concern to masculinize its song book. In this, perhaps more than in any other factor, we find the roots of the complaint by so many former members that the community is too rigid, legalistic, and stifling. Reason is reduced to ordered outlines and algorithms. Love is reduced to loyalty and ordered service. Spirituality is reduced to "being a good brother or sister in the community." And spiritual interiority is reduced to living submissively according to community order. Communities of this sort cannot become integral parts of Holy Mother Church, for motherhood is foreign to their very essence.

The teachings and practices of these communities can be seen to solve the significant problems in family life in contemporary culture. As both People of Praise and Sword of the Spirit developed, their leaders intended to offer an alternative to the way family life is ordered—or disordered—in our society. Their principal villain was feminist ideology and the kind of communal fracturing that we commonly see, by which neighbors often do not know each other, where friends often live too far away to visit on foot, where family life is often fragmented. Living in community was intended to address most of these problems. Indeed, we in the People of Praise often tried to live in "clusters" of households, usually under the headship of a community leader.

In fact, the problems of families and issues regarding the sexes are severe in contemporary Western societies. Most nations in the developed world are in a demographic free fall, because their citizens are not having enough children to maintain their populations.[235] Our Western culture is losing its ability to make sense of human sexual identity. One hears of "toxic masculinity" and conflicted notions of what constitutes a person as female, as experts, commentators, and ordinary people try to sort out the relationship between biological sex and gender. These issues give rise to serious problems, as young men and women marry later or not even at all, unsure of what their roles should be as husband and wife. We hear of "mommy wars" that manifest real perplexities among women as they sort out the priorities they seek (or should seek) for career in relation to motherhood. The covenant communities offer solutions to these problems, solutions that are in some respects heavy-handed and in others inadequate. Masculinity is not constituted by playing poker and firing muzzle-loaded pistols, while refusing to change dirty diapers. Nevertheless, even as we may reject the positions of the People of Praise and Sword of the Spirit, we continue to be faced with the inadequacies of most contemporary approaches.

CHAPTER 8.
CONCLUSIONS

We may draw some valuable conclusions, both negative and positive, from this study.

A. Negative

Both the Sword of the Spirit and the People of Praise are a danger to the faith of Catholics. Furthermore, the principles on which they are structured are sufficiently problematic that any group modeled upon them stands in danger of drifting away from an authentic Catholic life and falling into genuine abuses. This caveat can apply even to those groups which may enjoy some kind of official recognition by the local Ordinary.

Both People of Praise and Sword of the Spirit supplant the Church in the lives of their members. Even though they refuse to call themselves churches and even encourage their members to maintain membership in other churches, in appearance, structure, and function they resemble denominations. Indeed, we have seen that community membership purportedly establishes a special relationship with the Lord, a relationship that other Catholics do not share. Both community systems refer to themselves as "the Body of Christ." The Word of God is so named because of a prophetic promise at its inception that the community based in Ann Arbor was God's Word, spoken to the state of Michigan.

The claim by the Sword of the Spirit's and People of Praise to be organizations for Church renewal must be rejected. In fact, both systems have disengaged themselves as much as possible from the life of the Church on the parish and diocesan levels. Each relates to the Catholic Church (as well as the mainline Protestant denominations) precisely as a mere institution providing devotional and sacramental services. Neither People of Praise nor Sword of the Spirit has as its goal to promote or foster a deepening of sacramental and liturgical life. Nor do they foster a greater realization or living awareness of the fundamentally communal nature of the parish. Indeed, parish life is disdained. While purportedly promoting the life in the Holy Spirit, neither fosters a Spirit-filled devotion to Our Lady. Except to foster their own communities, they do not promote the New Evangelization so ardently promoted by Pope John Paul II, nor do they foster genuine ecumenical dialogue and theological reflection. Especially important is that these communities do not exist to promote or encourage personal holiness. Frequently leaders will teach that the primary mission of the community is simply to *be* who they are, that the very existence of the community is itself their greatest apostolic fruit.

Spokespersons for both groups have appealed to the Vatican II *Decree on the Apostolate of the Laity*, to John Paul II's *Christifideles Laici*, and to related documents that promote the freedom of the laity to form various apostolic organizations. Indeed, the Church explicitly allows and encourages Catholics to join with Christians of other church organizations to undertake charitable and apostolic works, although such organizations may not call themselves Catholic. Indeed, the new Code of Canon Law provides flexible guidelines for the formation of lay associations. This is all true, and this freedom is to be eagerly embraced and used. However, these freedoms must be understood in context and according to the mind of the Church. Specifically, the Church is very clear on the nature, source and locus of Christ's pastoral ministry. No group of lay persons may select, appoint, discern or recognize lay pastors from within its midst. Nowhere is suggested that lay people are permitted or much less competent to establish a local Christian community without the cooperation, much less the permission of the local Ordinary. Furthermore, it should be mentioned that neither the Vatican nor any local Ordinary has recognized either Sword of the Spirit or People of Praise as a Canonical Association of Christ's Lay Faithful.

We have tried to show the deleterious effects that these groups have on the individual's faith in the long run. Lacking the means of real grace and growth, they create a climate of sensible grace which after a few years begins to leave one feeling empty, frustrated, vaguely guilty and spiritually a failure. These groups lack the resources to bring one to the mystical encounter with Christ in suffering, which is constitutive of any genuine spirituality. The covenant community spirituality lacks any true depth. To grow spiritually the member simply needs to follow the recipe. The result has been in some cases that former members leave the Church. In many other cases they come out badly disillusioned and unwilling to risk such hurt again. Many have become deeply mistrustful of any renewal movement. The communities themselves can offer their suffering members nothing more than the exhortation to integrate their lives more fully with that of the group—to "jump in with both feet"—and not to expect any spiritual consolations.

Throughout her history, the Church has confronted spiritual movements and initiatives that, because of their zeal, purity of intention, strictness of life or manifest virtues offer what the Church seems to have lost. The Pelagian, Donatist, Jansenist, and Albigensian movements were all attractive, especially for those who were seeking a more perfect life in Christ.[236] Repeatedly the Church has had to condemn the errors of groups and movements which claimed to represent a more perfect way, and she has strenuously warned her children to avoid such groups.

In my opinion, it is appropriate and necessary for the bishops of the Church to take a formal concern regarding People of Praise, Sword of the Spirit and similar groups. Specifically, theologians need to study and evaluate the evidence and arguments presented in this paper, and the bishops advised of their findings. I recommend that, should those findings agree with those enumerated here, the bishops mandate immediate and radical reforms, in both the People of Praise and Sword of the Spirit, carefully supervised by priests and experts of the bishop's choosing. If either of these organizations refuse to comply, or if their compliance is marked by obstructionism, "stonewalling," foot dragging and other such ploys, the concerned bishops should take action. It would be appropriate for them to announce formally and publicly that the group is a danger to the faith, that Catholic members should leave it, and that others should not join. Community leaders have argued and will argue that because these communities are outside the Catholic Church, the bishops have no authority over them. However, most of their members are Catholic and, as has been shown earlier, their local bishops are indeed responsible for pastoring them.

B. Positive

The intense degree of commitment and the willingness to sacrifice which are manifested by so many members of these communities constitute a sign of hope for the Church. Let us consider this in some detail.

- a. *The longing for community:* Community members have taken concrete life-changing steps to realize a level of sharing of Christian life characteristic of the primitive Church. They wanted to see the Church alive and vibrant in such a way that their neighbors could indeed say "See how they love one another."
- b. *Eagerness to serve*: The willingness of covenant com-

munity members to serve the Lord and their fellow man is truly impressive. This "servant's heart" has made possible huge charismatic conferences, as well as care for brothers and sisters in community.

c. *Appreciation of authority*: While much has been said about allegations of abuse of authority, the genuine concern to respect and appreciate authority has seldom been noticed. Community members show that Catholics will respond well to leaders who ask concrete sacrifice and commitment of them for the sake of Christ.

d. *Love of God*: Most important, these communities reveal to us an immense desire to love God, to "give it all for Jesus." More than anything else, most members have joined their covenant communities to find a concrete way to live out this love for God.

These positive signs suggest the elements of a pastoral plan, indeed, not only for community members but for the Church. Catholics need a sense of belonging, that they are a valued part of a Church that accepts them. This is not to be understood in a static sense, as though everyone needs a club or family to derive his identity from. Rather it is a dynamic, missionary reality; to belong to the Catholic Church is to participate in an important mission, the mission of bringing salvation to the world. The Church calls us to holiness, which means to be saints, and to rise above the material concerns of this world. The Church must present this invitation clearly and concretely.

Lay persons have gifts to offer, and this is to be recognized. It is significant that although the founders of these communities had tried several times, they were not successful in establishing communities until the charismatic movement broke out. This may well have to do with the fact that most charismatics saw community as a setting where their spiritual gifts could be recognized, fostered, developed and put to good use in the service of the Church. Even if these communities stifle the individual's gifts in fact, their promise was that they will foster them. This is attractive. If lay persons know that their distinctive personal creativity and initiative are welcomed in the local Church and that they really can contribute something of value, then they will often respond enthusiastically. And by "gifts" we mean not just the extraordinary charismatic gifts, but the more natural gifts as well.

The Church must unabashedly proclaim the truth. In the 1970s, when covenant communities arose and enjoyed their greatest growth and success, one frequently heard blatant heresy from the pulpit, in the confessional, and in Catholic publications. Some priests denied the miracles of Christ and his bodily resurrection. Penitents were told that because God is love, fornication was not sinful "if you really care about each other." The founders of these communities were clearly, often forcefully, orthodox in their statements and defense of the fundamentals of the faith and the moral order. The fact is that in the 1970s the covenant community *seemed* to be the only place where the truths of the faith were unabashedly proclaimed, where holiness of life was really sought. As one member said when he joined the People of Praise, "It's the only game in town." There is a widespread belief in the United States that the truths of the Gospel must be softened, watered down and made palatable if the laity are to accept them. In fact, however, a clear proclamation of the truth will win committed Catholics with genuine zeal. Indeed, we might start winning new Christians.

It is vital to recapture solid devotion to Our Lady. There are two reasons for this. First, a religious expression that ignores Mary risks becoming masculinized. This has manifestly occurred in the covenant communities, where military imagery is prevalent and where women have been reduced to subservience. Second, Mary is the Mother and Model of the Church. To know her is to know the Church. "Mary is the beginning and the image of the Church as the bride of the new covenant."[237] The quickest and easiest way to instill a love for the Church and a sense for her true nature is to foster a solid Marian spirituality.

I say all this not so primarily as a scholar but as a witness. In 1984 my employer, Charismatic Renewal Services, sent me to Rome for three months to help administer the Worldwide Priests Retreat, which was sponsored by international charismatic organizations. There, on our own without the support of our "brothers and sisters" in community, Marie and I, with our four children, lived our lives. I worked and Marie taught the three older children. Although none of us knew much Italian beyond *buon giorno, grazie* and a few other tourist phrases we did well art navigating our daily life. The children thrived. As for me, I could pray my rosary on the bus and walk from our office over to St. Peter's Basilica to pray. One Tuesday our family could attend Pope John Paul II's daily audience, and then at the papal Mass we were seated several rows behind Mother Teresa of Calcutta. On Sundays we attended Mass in a lovely Franciscan church near our apartment. In Rome, I fell in love with the Church.

We must renew reverence for the Eucharist and a sacrificial understanding of it. Ironically, the tendency to treat the Eucharist as a "family meal" and to speak of sharing the "Jesus Bread" probably resulted in less sense of community rather than more, for there is no sense of common sharing in something truly sublime. The contemporary turn of so many—especially the young—to the Traditional Latin Mass is a sign for the Church to recapture the reality that the Mass is above all a Sacrifice, that self-same sacrifice as that which Christ offered. We need to recapture that sense of awe that the Lord himself has come to us through the action of the priest, and in doing so to rediscover the sense in which the priest is *alter Christus* ("another Christ"). While Eucharistic devotion in and of itself may not be sufficient to bring about an experience of community, it is a prerequisite and a strong impetus towards it. In the

Real Presence of Christ the Lord, all our earthly divisions are broken down, and we are united in him.

Let us strive to renew confidence in the Catholic faith. In our post-conciliar eagerness to rid the Church of triumphalism and a ghetto mentality, we have too often adopted a very reticent way of speaking about the Church's nature and prerogatives. Thus we may speak of ourselves as "Catholic Christians," an expression intended to lessen claims of exclusivity, but which tends to reduce the Catholic Church to the status of merely another denomination of Christians. Too often Catholic tradition is discussed in a way that suggests that ours is but one of many traditions, all more or less equally valid. The overall effect is that for the most part young Catholics do not regard the Church as the authoritative voice for Christ, much less as the means he has provided for us to know and serve him in love. In particular, one sees a reluctance, often fostered by religious educators, to accept the Church as the privileged or authoritative interpreter of Scripture. As a result, young Catholics are particularly vulnerable to the interpretations of powerful, eloquent and intelligent Bible teachers.

Finally, I am convinced that the teachings of Popes John Paul II and Benedict XVI should be faithfully disseminated. In the mid-1980s a survey of young people in Austria showed that although they liked the John Paul II, they wished he would talk about something other than sex all the time. However, the Popes talk very often about many other things than sex—including in their addresses to young people. In the United States one hears the complaint that the Church bans artificial contraception but will not offer convincing reasons why. Yet Pope John Paul II's series of audiences on the "theology of the body" included some very penetrating discussions of just this subject. Compared to the teachings of our modern popes, as well as other prominent Catholics—I may mention Bishop Fulton J. Sheen and St. John Henry Newman—the writings of Steven B. Clark are thin gruel indeed!

The People of Praise and the Sword of the Spirit have fallen into serious errors. Indeed, their very conception of themselves as Christian communities is fatally flawed. Nevertheless, the impulse which led many people to enter them was genuinely Christian and can be a wonderful resource for the Church. A proper response by the Church can not only avert a great danger to the faith of many but could even result in rich fruit for the Kingdom of God.

C. What Went Wrong

Having surveyed the foundational documents and the publications of these groups and their founders, we have identified much of what went wrong. Furthermore, we have discovered certain principles by which other, similar groups may be evaluated. At this point I want to highlight two fundamental themes that underlie most of the problems. These two themes are (i) the integrity and autonomy of the person and (ii) the nature of the Church.

Both covenant community systems have, in fact, so structured themselves that the individual person *qua* person is lost. The principal agent of mission and the principal subject of holiness is the community itself. The individual is constantly urged in teachings and especially by the culture that the community fosters to rely not on his own judgment and gifts but on the discernment of the leaders. He comes to feel strongly and often oppressively the call to deny himself, for that call eventually becomes not a challenge to give of himself in love, but to deny the self (or the person) that he is. If the teachings at the highest levels of a community may be nuanced so that freedom and autonomy are recognized in principle, at the grass-roots level they are denied. One has only to listen to the sharings and testimonies at a large community gathering to see this. Invariably, one's head is the one who gave proper direction to his life, and true peace was found only "when I stopped rebelling and listened to my head." Thus the individual becomes either alienated from the group with which he is to identify (in which case he leaves), or he becomes alienated from himself.

What makes this dilemma especially poignant is that the community is typically the member's experience of Christian community. The message communicated by the life itself of the community is that outside the group is dryness and death. The Church is "weak, confused and divided,"[238] unable to support an authentic Christian life. In fact, we have seen that both systems of communities tacitly assume that the denominational churches and the Catholic Church are, in a practical sense, religious organizations providing sacramental and liturgical services. They are regarded as communities only by a kind of fiction. In a very real sense, then, it is denied that what the member wants most, the reason he joined the community, can be found at all in the Church. But if he comes to find himself alienated from the community, he really has no hope. Individualism is inadequate, but his social experience of Christianity has proved destructive.

The great dichotomy between the individual and the collective is perfectly overcome in the Church. This is not to say that the Church is devoid of conflict, abuse of power, ambition, and the like. Obviously it is not. In as much as the Church is peopled by sinners, their sins are found in it. However, the Church is also divine, and her divine sociology perfectly overcomes the tension between person and society.

The life of the Church flows from the communion within the Blessed Trinity.[239] Father and Son are united in a perfect Love whose name is the Holy Spirit. The Church's unity flows from this unity. "The essential source of the Church's unity is also found in God the Trinity."[240] This Holy Spirit, which is the love between Father and Son and which constituted the assembly of the disciples as the Church on Pentecost, is given to each Christian person, making him or her a temple of the Holy Spirit.

This is the great truth we learn from those texts (Jn. 14:23; 15-16; 1 Cor. 3:16; Rom. 8:9, etc.): the human person is, in the Church, the dwelling place of God the Trinity and the whole Church, composed of persons in whom the Trinity dwells, is in its entirety the temple of the Trinity.[241]

The destiny of the Church, the Bride of Christ, is to become the New Jerusalem in which Christ, the Lamb that was slain, will be the light. The destiny of each individual Christian is to enjoy for all eternity the Beatific Vision, the intimate knowledge of and fellowship with God himself. Our perfect happiness, which is profoundly personal,[242] coincides with the eschatological realization of the reality of the Church.

This eschatological perspective sheds a significant light on our earthly situation. That which makes us Christian and by which we are "successful" as Christians is not our external condition or situation in the Church, regarded as a society. Rather, our condition as Christians depends on our interior relationship with God. To be sure, this has moral and social ramifications, but one's relationship with God and his Church is not constituted morally or socially. The Christian's response to God is therefore not merely a response as to an external authority, whether a community coordinator or the Pope. It is, rather, a response to One who is most intimate to him and Who is the Object of his deepest love and longing. Theology shows and history proves that one's holiness can be quite independent of that of others or of the condition of church institutions. Indeed, we may well say that the history of the Church is not the history of her institutions nor of her hierarchy but of her saints—that is, of her holy ones.

The communities have neglected this. To put the matter most bluntly, neither the Sword of the Spirit nor the People of Praise has ever articulated an account of grace. Neither community system relies on grace. The arrogation by systems of headship or pastoral care of the Holy Spirit's prerogative to instruct and convict intrudes upon the intimate relationship with God, which must constitute the core of the Christian life and experience.

A further point, albeit a subsidiary one, is that the Holy Spirit allocates gifts or charisms to the Church as he wills. These are for the Church, to be discerned by her Pastors.[243] For the member of the covenant community, these gifts are to be discerned by leadership of the community. Were this leadership under the authority of the Church's pastors, then these charisms would be at the service of the Church. However, since the communities are self-contained and not accountable to the Church, those gifts which the Holy Spirit would give through these individuals are effectively cut off from the whole of the Church.

Typically, the member who has left the covenant community testifies to an experience of freedom. This freedom arises not from a removal of exterior constraint but from the newly discovered right to respond to that which is within oneself. No longer does he require the approval of his head or a confirmation that his heart's desire conforms to the mission of the community. The gift of wisdom imparted by the Holy Spirit of God can again empower him to act in love and for the good of the Church.

The Church for her part becomes much more than an organization, an external society ruled by priests, bishops and the Pope. The Church can be known as Mother. Modeled on Mary, the Church brings Christians to birth in Baptism, nurtures and nourishes them with the Sacraments, instructs them with God's word, prods them with her moral teaching and encourages them with the example of the saints who have gone before. The Church is not an organization that needs a new kind of covenant to bring community into her midst. The Church *is* the Body of Christ, the community of those who believe. The Church is a communion that lives by the very life of God. It is the communion of the Blessed Trinity.

I want to conclude by emphasizing that our one and holy Church is called to be, and is placed on the world as, a revelation of that love which is God. The Church … is thus the 'sacrament of Trinitarian love'. Her most profound mystery consists precisely in this love. [244]

AFTERWORD:
A PERSONAL NOTE TO FORMER MEMBERS

To leave the covenant community, or to be dismissed from one, is a traumatic affair. You cannot stop talking about it. When Marie and I left People of Praise, we joined with some other former members to find a way forward. We were even encouraged by our local bishop to do this, to help each other out in this way and to find out how we might serve the Church going forward. Unfortunately, whenever we met, our conversation was almost entirely about our grievances with the community. Although it was hard not to talk about it, we realized that we needed to find a way forward, a way that was not built on the community *nor on a response to it.*

Marie, my wife came up with a strategy that helped her greatly and eventually helped me. She decided to find somebody *normal* in the parish and to see what she does. So she found Jane, whom we knew through the school that our children attended. Once a month Holy Cross School had "Bun Day", on which moms went to the school to serve sloppy joe's to the pupils. It was popular with the children and afforded the mothers good time to interact and build up friendships. So, Marie began to build her friendship with Jane and other moms in the parish. Indeed, we both found ourselves more deeply involved in parish life, as well as finding more ways to find activities with the children. We made a conscious effort to be normal and not *weird*.

An important step, especially for me, was repentance for participation in what the community had done. This book has argued throughout that the People of Praise, as well as Sword of the Spirit, was a spiritually illegitimate institution that supplants the role of the Church. Therefore, to participate in it was wrong. Having realized this, we both took the making of the covenant and our participation in the community life to confession, to ask God's forgiveness for our role—for my exercise of headship, for neglect of relatives, for participation in deliverance sessions, for a superior attitude toward other Christians. This repentance and confession were important to our freedom. It was very easy to blame our leaders for lying, manipulating and misleading us in many ways, Our marriage and family did really suffer. However, we were a part of this system and participated in it. It was not enough to recognize the wrongs done by our leaders. Frankly, I am ashamed and embarrassed.

Let me cite an apt secular example. From the end of World War II until 1990, Czechoslovakia suffered under the yoke of a Communist regime imposed by the Soviet Union, a totalitarian regime that denied ordinary freedoms to its people and instituted a reign of fear that permeated the ordinary lives of the people. At the end of 1989, the regime fell peacefully as the people were finally able to choose their own leaders. For the Presidency they elected a former dissident playwright and essayist, Václav Havel, who had suffered imprisonment and humiliation under the Communists. On New Year's Day, 1990, he addressed the nation as its now President. He began that talk by celebrating the new-found freedom and briefly summarizing what the Communist regime had done to harm Czechoslovakia. There was much harm and many people to blame. However, after mentioning these things, Havel pivoted to address the state of his fellow citizens, the people who enthusiastically elected him. He called them to a kind of national repentance. The newly free Czechoslovakia's President said,

> But all this is still not the main problem. The worst thing is that we live in a contaminated moral environment. We fell morally ill because we became used to saying something different from what we thought. ... When I talk about a contaminated moral atmosphere ... I am talking about all of us. We had all become used to the totalitarian system and accepted it as an unchangeable fact and thus helped to perpetuate it. In other words, we are all—though naturally to differing extents—responsible for the operation of the totalitarian machinery; none of us is just its victim: we are all also its co-creators.[245]

The central issue for Czechoslovakia's people was that they had been living a lie. Havel's solution was, in effect, to live not by lies.

Our situation—here I am speaking to the consciences of those of us who have lived in covenant community—is that we have lived a lie, a structural falsehood that distorted our understanding of Christ's Church and his plan for our lives. But Jesus is marvelously patient and disconcertingly forgiving. If we have followed a wrong path, he does not hold it against us. He dies on the cross for love of us. And what he wants of us is to live that love and to love our neighbors, whom he came to save. The Church is marvelously adaptable to personalities and cultures. In the fifth century St. Benedict wanted to live his life free from the temptations of the world, and after several unsuccessful attempts he gathered some brothers and gave them a rule to live by. This resulted in the establishment of the Abbey at Monte Cassino and, indeed, the entire monastic movement, which endures to this day. Six centuries later, St. Francis renounced all his family's wealth and undertook to live in radical poverty. The Franciscans were not monks, living in a monastery but itinerant preachers. Franciscans continue to this day, while the order has developed different offshoots to meet different needs of the Church and the world. We could go on to talk about Jesuits, the orders and other apostolic works that sprang up in France after the French Revolution, the work of St. Maximilian Kolbe to spread devotion to Mary, and many other initiatives in the Church. The Christian who wants to serve God has unlimited options, if he or she is willing to act in truth and in love. Everyone who leaves a covenant community can serve God and witness to his neighbor what God has done. In you have left a community, you have opened a door that has kept you from fulfilling God's plan for your life.

The People of Praise and the Sword of the Spirit sprang up in a time of misguided pastoral experimentation, liturgical silliness, and theological confusion in the wake of the Second Vatican Council. The vision of the four principal founders was of a perfect Church built up of fully committed communities of loyal Christians. In a time of ecumenical expectations fostered by the Council, their communities were to be founded on the common understanding of Christ embraced by all Christians in communities whose members love each other and God in good order and spiritual discipline. When he called for the Second Vatican Council, Pope John XXIII had hoped for a renewal of the Church by the Holy Spirit. Although these communities arose from within the charismatic renewal movement, they ignored the role of "those who are appointed leaders in the Church, to those whose special competence it belongs, not indeed to extinguish the Spirit, but to test all things and hold fast to what is good (cf. 1 Thess. 5:12, 19-21)." [246] The Church has survived bad leaders, schisms, and heresies, and the Holy Spirit has always raised up saints to renew her. However, no matter how bad things may be—and historically they have gotten very bad at times—she does not need us to replace her with ill-formed groups led by ill-informed leaders.

ENDNOTES

1 As will become clear in the text, what began as The Word of God community eventually became the Sword of the Spirit, from which The Word of God split off as a different kind of organization.

2 Mathilde de Robien, "Pourquoi le Vatican ordonne un visite apostolique au sein de la Communauté de l'Emmanuel?", *Aletheia,*. Downloaded 2 November 2025 from https://fr.aleteia.org/2025/10/28/pourquoi-le-vatican-ordonne-une-visite-apostolique-au-sein-de-la-communaute-de-lemmanuel/?utm_medium=email&utm_source=sendgrid&utm_campaign=EM-FR-Newsletter-WeeklySunday-&utm_content=Newsletter&utm_term=20251102.

3 *Veritatis Splendor,* §17.

4 These are elements of the original covenant of the People of Praise.

5 National Conference of Catholic Bishops, *A Pastoral Statement on the Catholic Charismatic Renewal* (Washington, C.D., 1989) § 13.

6 See James LeBar, *Cults, Sects and the New Age,* (OSV OSV Press, Huntington, Ind., 1989). Adrian J. Reimers, "Covenant Community: A failed promise," *Fidelity*, May 1986 (subsequently reprinted in *Cultic Studies Journal*, Vol. 3, #1, Spring-Summer 1986). *The National Catholic Register* ran a series of articles on covenant communities from April until August, 1992, in which many of these charges were brought forward. For an early treatment by a theologian, see Josephine M. Ford, *Which Way for Catholic Pentecostals* (Harper & Row, New York, 1976), which quite accurately predicted many of the problems that have arisen.

7 The reader will need to know some history to understand what is being referred to here. What presently exists as the Sword of the Spirit was founded in 1969 as The Word of God (WOG) in Ann Arbor, Michigan. In 1981 the Sword of the Spirit was founded as a network or community of communities, of which WOG was the first. Then in 1990 WOG effectively split off from Sword of the Spirit, abandoning many of the latter's practices and beliefs. In particular, The Word of God introduced the election of leaders, and it abolished its "pastoral system." Thus the pre-1981 WOG is continuous with Sword of the Spirit, and the post-1990 WOG is a significantly different organization. Because the "new" Word

of God community continues to undergo radical reform, a critique of it is simply not possible at this time. Therefore, this essay does not discuss that organization.

8 Two noteworthy examples not inspired by the South Bend - Ann Arbor models are the Community of God's Delight (Dallas, Texas) and the young people's community founded by Fr. Richard Rohr O.F.M. in Cincinnati, Ohio.

9 "Prophecies given at St. Peter's Basilica During the Closing Eucharist on Pentecost Monday,"*New Covenant*, July 1975, p. 26.

10 Rev. Kilian McDonnell, OSB, *The Charismatic Renewal and Ecumenism*, (Servant, Ann Arbor, 1978), p. 111-112.

11 Stephen B. Clark, *Training Program*, Talk #1, "What Is This War Anyway?"

12 Pius XII, *Mystici corporis, A.A.S.XXXV*, pp. 199, 223-224. See also John Paul II, Apostolic Exhortation, *Christifideles laici*, sec. 19, 24, 26; Encyclical, *Redemptoris missio*, Sec. 51; audience of November 20, 1991.

13 Pius XII, op. cit., pp. 221-222.

14 *Redemptoris missio*, Sec 51.

15 Congregation for the Doctrine of the Faith, (Joseph Cardinal Ratzinger, Prefect and Most Rev. Albert Bovone), *The Church Understood as Communion*, sec. 6. See also Joseph Ratzinger, *The Open Circle: The Meaning of Christian Brotherhood* (Sheed & Ward, New York, 1966), pp. 100 f.

16 John Paul II, *Redemptor hominis*, Sec. 20.

17 Significantly, the Second Vatican Council's Decree on Ecumenism, *Unitatis redintegratio*, sec. 2, finds precisely in this the foundation of true ecumenism.

18 *Redemptor hominis*, sec. 20.

19 Dogmatic Constitution on the Church, *Lumen Gentium*, Chapter 1, sec. 3. See also *Redemptor hominis*, sec. 20. And John Paul II, Audience of September 11, 1991.

20 Congregation for the Doctrine of the Faith, Op. cit., sec. 17.

21 Second Vatican Council, Decree on the Ministry and Life of Priests, *Presbyterorum ordinis*, n. 6

22 John L. McKenzie, S.J., *Dictionary of the Bible*, (Macmillan Co., New York, 1965), "Covenant," p. 153.

23 John Paul II, General Audience of 20 July 1991.

24 Joseph Ratzinger, *Behold the Pierced One*, Ignatius Press, San Francisco, 1986, pp. 84-85.

25 Ratzinger, *The Open Circle*, pp. 80, 100.

26 When the People of Praise was praying about its name, the next preferred contender—after "People of Praise"—was "Family of Faith."

27 See John Paul II, General Audience of 31 March 1993.

28 Constitution on Sacred Liturgy, *Sacrosanctum concilium*, Sec. 41

29 John Paul II, Apostolic Exhortation, *Christifideles laici*, 23. See Vatican II, Decree on the Ministry and Life of Priests, *Presbyterorum ordinis*, 2 and 5.

30 *The Code of Canon Law*, can. 215.

31 Decree on the Apostolate of Lay People, *Apostolicam actuositatem*, 3.

32 *Presbyterorum ordinis*, 2 and 5.

33 Ratzinger and Bovone, op. cit. sec 6.

34 Ratzinger, *The Open Circle*, p. 102.

35 *Lumen gentium*, 12

36 Especially helpful is Libero Geroso's discussion in *Charisma und Recht: Kirchenrechtliche Überlegungen zum "Urcharisma" der neuen Vereinigungsformen in der Kirche* (Johannes Verlag, Einsiedeln, Trier, 1989), pp. 96-105.

37 Memo of September 2, 1964, page 4. The emphasis is added.

38 ibid. p. 1.

39 ibid. p. 6.

40 Stephen B. Clark, *Building Christian Communities (BCC)*, p. 82.

41 ibid. p. 53.

42 ibid. p. 139.

43 ibid. p. 22. See also J. Ford, op. cit., pp. 8-12.

44 Stephen B. Clark, *Unordained Elders and Renewal Communities* p. 58.

45 ibid. p. 7.; also *Building Christian Communities* p. 139.

46 St. Thomas Aquinas, *De Veritate* q. 27, a. 3 and a. 4.

47 Clark, *Building Christian Communities*, pp. 141-142.

48 Minutes, "General Council Meeting," August 8-10, 1977. For more on the Council, see Chapter V of this essay.

49 Stephen Clark, Memo to: Paul DeCelles, Kevin Ranaghan, Ralph Martin, Jim McFadden, Bruce Yocum, July 18, 1977.

50 ibid.

51 This rejection of medieval Scholastic thought surfaces again, albeit obliquely, in Clark's *Covenant Community and Church,* (Servant Publications, Ann Arbor, 1992) p. 23.

52 It should be noted that the People of Praise, too, holds up discipleship as its model for intellectual formation, even if their practice of it is haphazard. In particular, the community's "Building Blocks of Christian Culture" teaching series contains one presentation on training and advocates discipleship as a model. The relationship of "full-life submission" to one's personal pastor was long regarded as a prerequisite for growth to full spiritual maturity in that group.

53 John Paul II, *Pastores dabo vobis*, secs. 51 ff.

54 ibid., sec. 52.

55 John Paul II, Encyclical *Fides et Ratio*, §23.

56 Cf. John Paul II: "Theology is nothing other than the intellectual analysis of the mysteries of the Trinity, Incarnation and Redemption." "In-flight Remarks to Journalists," *L'Osservatore Romano* (English Edition) No. 8 - 26 Feb. 1992, p. 12.

57 Clark is reported to have been an enthusiastic student of Ludwig Wittgenstein. If this is so, then Wittgenstein's dictum about language, "Don't look for meaning. Look for use," fits his conception well.

58 See Stephen Arterburn and Jack Felton, *Toxic Faith*, (Oliver Nelson, Nashville, 1991); David Johnson and Jeff VanVonderen, *The Subtle Power of Spiritual Abuse*, (Bethany House, Minneapolis, 1991), and especially Ronald M. Enroth, *Churches that Abuse*, Zondervan, Grand Rapids, 1992. For a Catholic analysis, see Rev. James LeBar, *Cults, Sects and the New Age*, and *Sects or New Religious Movements: A Pastoral Challenge*, The Vatican Report.

59 For an excellent account and analysis, see Edward D. O'Connor, C.S.C., *The Pentecostal Movement in the Catholic Church* (Ave Maria Press, Notre Dame, Indiana, 1971).

60 "The Charter of the Sword of the Spirit," in Constitution of the Sword of the Spirit, 6/89.

61 "Our Ecumenical Approach," Constitution of the Sword of the Spirit, ID1.3

62 From the Constitution of Sword of the Spirit. The numbering of sentences is not in the original, but is added here for convenience of reference.

63 See Exodus 34: 10 ff.; Jeremiah 24: 7; Isaiah 42: 6; 43: 1; 44: 24; 49: 8.

64 The Dogmatic Constitution on the Church *"Lumen Gentium," Sec. 1.*

65 Rom. 6: 3-4; also *Lumen gentium*, Sec. 7.

66 Pope John Paul II, *Christifideles laici*, sec. 12

67 "Technically, the diocese is the local Church," remarks Clark in his *Building Christian Communities*, p. 66, but he then proceeds to argue that the diocese "cannot function like a real community."

68 *Lumen Gentium*, secs. 20-21. Pope John XXIII's comparison of the parish church with the village fountain at which all gather is apt here.

69 Clark, *Building Christian Communities*, p. 70.

70 Stephen Clark, *Knowing God's Will*, (Servant Books, Ann Arbor,1974) pp. 52-56.

71 Stephen B. Clark, *Patterns of Christian Community*, (Servant Books, Ann Arbor, 1984) pp. 63, 67-75.

72 ibid. p. 51.

73 ibid. p. 15.

74 Cf. Bruce Yocum, "A Response to John Haughey's Paper," *Theological Reflections on the Charismatic Renewal* (Edited by John C. Haughey, S.J., Servant Publications, Ann Arbor, Michigan, 1978), pp. 126-127.

75 Clark, *Unordained Elders and Renewal Communities*, p. 58. See also *Patterns of Christian Community*, p. 37.

76 Clark, *Building Christian Communities*, pp. 53, 67.

77 ibid., p. 39.

78 To be sure, the Church claims to be the body of Christ, a kind of sacrament, but it is also true that this is in a way independent of the social structure of any local body in the Church. Because Christ is substantially present in the Eucharist and dispenses His graces objectively through the Gospel as preached at Mass and through the sacraments, he is really present in the parish community even when the parish is "dead" and its pastor irresponsible. Pope John Paul II pointedly remarks on this score: "Plainly and simply, the Parish is founded on a theological reality, because it is a Eucharistic Community." John Paul II, *Christifideles laici*, Sec. 26.

79 Stephen B. Clark, *Man and Woman in Christ*, p. 256. For Clark's emphasis on Christianity as a social structure, see also pp. 224, 261 ff., and 275, among others.

80 ibid. 224.

81 ibid. p. 125, 575. This theme of "one person" occurs repeatedly in *Man*

and Woman in Christ. Husband and wife are to be "one person"; see pp. 83, 85, 180, and 262.

82 *Principles of Structure and Government of the People of Praise*, X-B-1.

83 "St. Gregory the Great on Pastoral Care," *National Catholic Register*, June 14, 1992.

84 Kevin Ranaghan, Address to the People of Praise, June 24, 1979.

85 *New Heaven/New Earth*, October 1991

86 *"The Spirit and Purpose of the People of Praise,"* sec. 2.

87 *New Heaven/New Earth*, July 1985.

88 J. M. Ford cites this as an important contact between these communities and the Radical Reformation, that their leaders claimed not "apostolic succession" but "apostolicity" or apostolic gifts and function. See Ford, op. cit. p. 45.

89 Joseph Ratzinger, *Behold the Pierced One*, pp. 75 ff.

90 John Paul II, General Audience of 11 September 1991; Homily in Goiania, Brazil, October 15, 1991.

91 John Paul II, *Redemptor hominis*, sec. 20.

92 "To these ends, (new members) receive instruction in fundamental truths of Christianity, personal holiness, formation in the Spirit, loving personal relationships and being a Christian in the modern world. Underway members should normally expect significant and specific changes in their way of life as they understand and put into practice the teachings of the community." *Spirit and Purpose*, 4 "Formation."

93 People of Praise, *Pastoral Guidelines*, pp. 16-19.

94 ibid. pp. 24 ff.

95 *"Spirit and Purpose,"* sec. 1

96 ibid. sec. 2.

97 ibid. sec. 5.

98 ibid. sec. 2.

99 Of course, the same could be said of the Orthodox.

100 People of Praise, *Pastoral Guidelines*, pp. 16-19.

101 Paul C. DeCelles, Teaching to coordinators' retreat, April 27-29, 1990.

102 *Spirit and Purpose*, sec. 5.

103 John Paul II, *Man and Woman He Created Them: A Theology of the Body*, 203.

104 *Presbyterorum ordinis*, 2; cf. *Lumen gentium*, 10 and John Paul II, *Pastores*

dabo vobis, sec. 15.

105 "For the Record: An Interview with Overall Coordinator Paul DeCelles Safeguards," *Vine and Branches*, April 1991, Vol. 7, no. 3.

106 The first version of the covenant of the People of Praise did state that the life of the community would be "in full harmony with the bishops and faithful of the Catholic Church." When a young Protestant man objected that he could not enter the community under this circumstance, that phrase was modified to "in full harmony with the Church."

107 The leaders and members of the People of Praise regularly refer to their organization as "the Body of Christ"; cf. K. Ranaghan's address of June 24, 1979.

108 Paul DeCelles, Address to the People of Praise, South Bend, February 21, 1993.

109 *Spirit and Purpose*, sec. 17

110 *Lumen gentium*, 30.

111 Paragraph XIII-A-1

112 Decree Concerning the Pastoral Office of Bishops in the Church *Christus Dominus*, *The Documents of Vatican II* (Boston: St Paul Publications, 2009), §2.

113 Pope Paul VI, *Humanae Vitae*(Vatican City: Libreria Editrice Vaticana, 1968).

114 It is worth noting that precisely the same thing is true of those groups described as "cults" or "mind-control" organizations. See Steven Hassan, *Combatting Cult Mind Control* (Park Street Press, Rochester, Vt. 1988), pp. 76 ff.

115 John Paul II, Address to leaders of the Catholic Fraternity of Covenant Communities, December 7,1991.

116 For a good example of this see Stephen Clark's *Knowing God's Will*. Also the *Pastoral Guidelines of the People of Praise*, pp. 24-28.

117 Clark's *Patterns of Christian Community* explicitly endorses "avoidance" or shunning. See p. 36. See also J. M. Ford, op. cit. pp. 58-60.

118 Msgr. James A. Boehm, "Bishop Ottenweller determines to correct abuses within local charismatic community," *The Steubenville Register*, Vol. 46, No. 19, Friday, June 21, 1991

119 Sword of the Spirit, "Council Decisions, 10/20/90, *The Relationship between The Sword of the Spirit and Christ the King Association*.

120 It is in this light that Stephen B. Clark's, *Covenant Community and Church* (Servant Books, Ann Arbor, 1992), must be read. In the "Preface"

Clark explains, "*Covenant Community and Church* was originally written as a draft document for the Christ the King Association, an international lay association of Catholics." As such it fails to mention much that is fundamental to the Sword of the Spirit, teachings and practices that are set forth in the group's constitution and in *Patterns of Christian Community*. The book is, in fact, a very general statement of principles, most of which would apply to just about any Catholic lay organization. Points of contact with Clark's previous writings and with the "Constitution of the Sword of the Spirit" are left vague or undefined.

121 John Paul II, Address to the Plenary Assembly of the Sacred Congregation for the Clergy, October 20, 1984.

122 In the late 70s a number of charismatic speakers began teaching about the distinction between God's "eternal word" or logos and his "now word" or rhema. As charismatics we were called to hear and respond to the rhema as well as the logos.

123 This was precisely Ranaghan's point in his address (mentioned above) on the "quitting spirit"; because God was doing a great work of healing and evangelization through the People of Praise at the time, Satan was attacking the group through the decisions of several members to leave.

124 This is precisely why St. John of the Cross warns of "spiritual gluttony" in his *Ascent of Mount Carmel*, in *The Collected Works of St. John of the Cross* (Washington, DC: ICS Publications, 2017) 182.

125 Constitution of the Sword of the Spirit, "Pastoral Approach," P. 5.

126 ibid. p. 3.

127 Obviously this is an idealized view of traditional society and the tribal village. Clark presents a vision and not the results of a scientific investigation. For his part, Paul DeCelles seemed to admire the village of Anatevka as represented in the film *Fiddler on the Roof* by Tevye's song "Tradition".

128 Clark, *Patterns of Christian Community*, p. 67.

129 See *Gaudium et Spes*, §§14-16.

130 On this see Karol Wojtyla (Pope John Paul II), *Person and Act*, (Washington, DC: The Catholic University Press, 2021), especially "Part Two: The Transcendence of the Person in the Act." See also K. Wojtyla "Thomistic Personalism," in *Person and Community*, (New York, San Francisco, Bern: Peter Lang, 1993), especially pp. 171 f.

131 Clark, *Patterns of Christian Community*, p. 17.

132 ibid. p. 51

133 Karol Wojtyla (John Paul II), *Person and Act*, pp. 380-381.

134 Paul DeCelles has also made exactly this point in teaching his own People of Praise.

135 See David Wilkerson, *The Cross and the Switchblade*, (Pueblo, CO: World Challenge, 2025)

136 This is well illustrated in, *To Serve as Jesus Served*, a book by People of Praise coordinator, Clem Walters, who suggests that the Christian envision himself standing before the Lord in chauffeur's livery, waiting for orders.

137 St. Thomas Aquinas, *Quaestiones de Veritate*, q. 23, a. 7.

138 Clark, *Patterns of Christian Community*, p. 61.

139 Stephen B. Clark, *Knowing God's Will*, Servant, Ann Arbor, 1974, p. 14. Compare Paul DeCelles' remarks in a teaching to the People of Praise in April 1978: "At the moment of decision, the Lord wants you to do ONE THING. The devil wants you to do anything else. It is a real battle."

140 In this context it is important to note the strong mistrust of emotion in the teachings and life of the Sword of the Spirit. See the "Report on the Harmful Effects of the Training Course" commissioned by the leaders of The Word of God community. Likewise in the People of Praise the emotions —especially women's emotions—are distrusted, and among the women there is a frequent appeal to "where you are in your cycle" in addressing "pastoral problems."

141 ibid. p. 61.

142 ibid. p. 63.

143 It should be noted that similar practices have occurred in the People of Praise.

144 Paul DeCelles, "For the Record Pastoral Care: Part I," *Vine and Branches*, November and December, 1989.

145 Letter, Dan DeCelles to P. P., dated November 17, 1989.

146 Paul DeCelles expressly acknowledges this dual role of the head in the above-mentioned articles on pastoral care.

147 *Spirit and Purpose*, sec. 15.

148 *Pastoral Guidelines of the People of Praise*, p. 16.

149 The minutes of coordinators' meetings of the People of Praise are quite striking in this regard. The term "pastor" is used regularly to mean "to influence" or "to get to obey." Thus: Sept. 27, 1985 - S. B. Branch Coordinators Mtg. "Kevin asked that we remind those we *pastor* to make their support

payments on a monthly basis." And: March 27, 1985 - Area Coordinators Meeting. "Ralph mentioned to us to continue to *pastor* those who need to pay Trinity tuition." Or: May 17, 1985 - Memo from Kevin Ranaghan to S. B. Branch Coordinators. "Sharing fund is low low low (sic)." Please continue to *pastor* the appeal I made at the last community meeting." Further: October 31, 1984 - Area Coordinators Mtg. "We reviewed some service placement assignments that have not been accepted. We decided to put some of these back on the list to be assigned, and others we want to check on through the *pastoral* system." May 11, 1984 - Memo to S.B. coordinators from Bob McDonough. "We also need to *pastor* the individual families in assuming their obligations to fund their children's education." This list could be expanded.

150 It should be noted that a *handmaid* in the People of Praise or Sword of the Spirit was nothing at all like the handmaids in Margaret Atwood's novel.

151 On one occasion, after we were out of the People of Praise, a young friend from Austria came to visit our home. Since she could not speak English, she asked our daughter, whose German is very good, to translate. Before doing so, Teresa was warned that she was as strictly bound by the seal of confession as the priest.

152 *Code of Canon Law*, Canon 240 - 2.

153 Paul DeCelles, "Going all out," *Pastoral Renewal*, Vol. 5, No. 2, August 1980.

154 Henri de Lubac, *The Motherhood of the Church*, (Ignatius Press, San Francisco 1982), p. 110.

155 *Pastoral Guidelines of the People of Praise*, p. 2.

156 *The Code of Canon Law* (1983), Can. 1172.

157 Cited in Paul Thigpen, *Manual for Spiritual Warfare*, Tan Books, Charlotte, NC, 2014.

158 *Pastoral Guidelines of the People of Praise*, p. 2.

159 St. John Paul II, Post-Synodal Apostolic Exhortation *Pastores Dabo Vobis*, downloaded from The Holy See, 27 June, 2025, https://www.vatican.va/content/john-paul-ii/en/apost_exhortations/documents/hf_jp-ii_exh_25031992_pastores-dabo-vobis.html

160 John 10: 1.

161 Clark, *Patterns of Christian Community*, p. 63.

162 The Apostles Creed for Sword of the Spirit and the Nicene Creed for People of Praise.

163 *Constitution of the Sword of the Spirit*, "Our Ecumenical Approach," ID1.1-6

164 A deutero-canonical book found in Catholic Bibles, but not in those

used by Protestants.

165 *Constitution of the Sword of the Spirit*, "Our Ecumenical Approach," ID1.3.

166 Second Vatican Council, Dogmatic Constitution on Divine Revelation *Dei Verbum*, §10.

167 *Spirit and Purpose*, sec. 16.

168 Second Vatican Council, Constitution on the Church, *Lumen Gentium*, §8.

169 *Lumen Gentium*, §§62-65.

170 *Redemptor hominis*, sec 20.

171 Minutes, "Meeting of the Council," September 8-10, 1974.

172 Minutes, General Council Meeting, August 8-10, 1977.

173 ibid.

174 Significantly, a subsequent note to the minutes observes, "Ralph and Steve are currently pessimistic over their relationship with the Cardinal."

175 Abp. Antonio Ambrosiano, "Only the ecumenism of truth can lead to fulness of unity," *L'Osservatore Romano*, (English edition), N. 38 - 23 September 1992.

176 In Sword of the Spirit Constitution, ID1.3

177 Dogmatic Constitution on Divine Revelation, *Dei verbum*, §10.

178 Decree on Ecumenism, *Unitatis redintegratio*, sec 2.

179 Significantly, in the minutes of the General Council Meeting, August 8-10, 1977, Kevin Ranaghan comments that CRS (Charismatic Renewal Services) is considering "banning communion until unity is restored." As Director of Conferences for CRS at the time, I had never heard such a proposal, but Ranaghan did see fit to bring it up in the context of the Council's discussion of unity.

180 See Rev. James LeBar, op. cit. Appendix VII, Letter from Johannes Cardinal Willebrands, President of the Secretariat for Christian Unity, to Archbishop Peter Gerety of Newark, New Jersey, dated April 2, 1986. "In this regard we would affirm your authority as Archbishop in matters concerning teaching, evangelization, spiritual formation and ecumenism in your Archdiocese." And later: "If Catholics join an ecumenical organization, the organization does not replace the jurisdiction of their bishop, who remains for Catholics the 'authentic teacher endowed with the authority of Christ' (*Lumen Gentium*, §25)."

181 Handmaids in the People of Praise were specially designated women whose job it was to support the husband's headship. Through the hand-

maid a woman could hear the voice of community leadership, especially when her husband proved ineffectual at this.

182 The People of Praise will allow a woman to hold an administrative position over a man, for instance in its outreach, Charismatic Renewal Services. However, there can never be a case of a woman's exercising pastoral governance over men.

183 People of Praise undated memo, "Caribbean Outreach."

184 John Paul II, *Man and Woman He Created Them: A Theology of the Body*

185 Available from Warhorn Media at https://mwc.warhornmedia.com/Man-and-Woman-in-Christ.pdf

186 Clark, *Man and Woman in Christ*, p. 261. See also ibid. p. 256 and 262.

187 ibid. p. 224.

188 ibid. p. 182.

189 This author experienced this dynamic in a life-changing way. Toward the end of a long conversation with Paul DeCelles in the summer of 1972, during which we discussed the structure of my relationship with my own wife, DeCelles read several of these passages from the New Testament, put down the Bible, looked up at me and simply asked, "Do you believe that?" Unwilling to resist God's truth, I accepted DeCelles's interpretation of these texts. It was not until about ten years later that I began to unravel the bind that this interpretation had put on our marriage. DeCelles's nephew, Dan DeCelles once related to me having had an almost identical experience with his uncle.

190 Clark, *Man and Woman in Christ*, "Note on Method: Exegesis," pp. 221-226.

191 Here we may note St. Teresa of Avila's comment to her sisters that, as religious sisters, they were fortunate not to be subject to the whims of aristocratic Spanish men, as so many of their married contemporaries were.

192 Clark, *Man and Woman in Christ*, p. 83.

193 ibid., p. 85.

194 Boethius, *De duabus naturis et una persona Christi*. See also, St. Thomas Aquinas, *Summa Theologiae I*, 29, 1 and Karol Wojtyla (Pope John Paul II), *Person and Act*, p. 176.

195 For interested readers, I am happy to argue that Aquinas was right.

196 Joseph Ratzinger, *Behold the Pierced One*, p. 92.

197 Bruce Yocum, "Pastoral Care in Sword of the Spirit," Address given June 5, 1991.

198 See Karol Wojtyła, *Love and Responsibility*, 28-29.

199 Indeed, one senior coordinator of the People of Praise did state in the early 70s that a good wife is like "a one-man dog." See Wendy Leifeld, "The Gender Issue, 2," *The National Catholic Register*, May 24, 1992.

200 *Man and Woman in Christ*, p. 649.

201 Vatican II, *Gaudium et Spes*, 17

202 Karol Wojtyla (Pope John Paul II) *Love and Responsibility*, (Farrar, Straus, Giroux; New York 1981), pp. 23-24.

203 In which the shared goods are the ends of marriage: procreation, mutual support, etc. See *Love and Responsibility*, p. 30, "These objective purposes of marriage *create in principle the possibility of love*." (emphasis added)

204 Wojtyla, *Love and Responsibility*, pp. 28-29

205 Clark, *Man and Woman in Christ*, p. 81.

206 John Paul II, *Man and Woman He Created Them*, 550.

207 *Man and Woman in Christ*, p. 488.

208 *Constitution of the Sword of the Spirit*, Community Weekend #3.

209 St. John of the Cross, *Dark Night of the Soul*, in *Collected Works of St. John of the Cross*.358-359.

210 St. Augustine, *Confessions*, (Image Books, Garden City, NY 1960), Book I, Chapter 1.

211 St. Thomas Aquinas, *Summa Theologiae, Ia, IIae* qq. 1-3.

212 We may add that this fact of itself structures their life anew with a fresh set of commitments!

213 David Crumm, "The Rise and Fall of a Heavenly Empire," *Detroit Free Press Magazine*, September 20, 1992, p. 14.

214 However, Clark acknowledges the help received from People of Praise leaders Kevin Ranaghan and Kerry Koller.

215 *Spirit and the Purpose*, sec. 10.

216 ibid. sec. 14.

217 John Paul II, *Man and Woman He Created Them*, 467-473

218 John Paul II, Apostolic Exhortation *Mulieris Dignitatem*, §29

219 We must note that Trinity School has undergone fundamental changes since it was founded and is now independent of the People of Praise, under the name Trinity Academy. It has existed in three different locations nationwide, and Trinity School in South Bend has now come

under independent governance (although this change seems to have resulted in two separate incarnations of the school, one of which is independent of People of Praise).

220 *Vine and the Branches*, "The Pastoral Care of Married Women": An Interview with Overall Coordinator Paul DeCelles, Volume 5, No. 7, August 1989, pp. 8-9.

221 ibid. p. 9.

222 One "head" within the People of Praise warned that one effect of original sin upon women is that they have become manipulative, even to the point of using theological or spiritual arguments as a "smokescreen." A wise husband will guard against this by drawing close to his head for counsel.

223 "The Pastoral Care of Married Women," p. 9

224 For more on this see my "Covenant Community: A Failed Promise," *Cultic Studies Journal*, Vol. 03, No. 01, 1986, pp. 36-56.

225 "The Pastoral Care of Married Women," p. 8.

226 John Paul II, *Man. And Woman He Created Them: A Theology of the Body*).

227 John Paul II notes that the Hebrew word "*adam*" means simply "human being."

228 *Man and Woman He Created Them*, p. 456.

229 Ibid. P. 473.

230 Vatican II, *Lumen gentium*, Ch. VIII, especially sec. 53, 63.

231 John Paul II, Encyclical, *Redemptoris Mater*, Part III, "Maternal Mediation."

232 John Paul II, *Mulieris Dignitatem*, Sec. 29

233 ibid. sec. 18

234 In the People of Praise, men were quietly taught by their heads and leaders not to change or rinse out diapers. In the Sword of the Spirit there have been cases of fathers calling neighboring women to come over to change the baby, when their own wives were not home.

235 Andrew Stanley, "Demographic Decline", F&D Magazine, September 2024, downloaded 18 November 2025 from https://www.imf.org/en/publications/fandd/issues/2024/09/picture-this-demographic-decline-andrew-stanley

236 The latter two movements, Jansenist and Albigensian, were criticized in depth in Ronald Knox's study *Enthusiasm* (Westminster, MD: Christian Classics, 1983). When it was suggested that Catholic charismatics

might well learn valuable lessons from Msgr. Knox, Dorothy Ranaghan, co-author (with her husband Kevin) of *Catholic Pentecostals*, dismissed the parallels as irrelevant to contemporary charismatics.

237 John Paul II, Audience of December 11, 1991. See too *Lumen gentium*, Chapter VIII.

238 A phrase repeated frequently by Ralph Martin at the 1976 Conference of Communities at the University of Notre Dame.

239 See J. Ratzinger, *Behold the Pierced One*, pp. 15 ff.

240 John Paul II, Audience of 9 October 1991.

241 ibid.

242 Karol Wojtyła, *The Lublin Lectures/Wykłady Lubelskie*, translated by Hugh McDonald, (Lublin: Polskie Towarzystwo Tomasza z Akwinu, 2020) 442-453.

243 Libero Gerosa, *Charisma und Recht*, Erstes Kapitel, III, 1.

244 John Paul II, Audience of 9 October 1991.

245 Václav Havel, *Open Letters* translated by Paul Wilson (London: Faber & Faber, 1991) 391-392.

246 Vatican II, Dogmatic Constitution on the Church *Lumen Gentium*, §14.

BIBLIOGRAPHY

Published Materials

Ambrosiano, Antonio. "Only the Ecumenism of Truth Can Lead to Fullness of Unity." *L'Osservatore Romano*, English edition, September 23, 1992.

Aquinas, Thomas. *Quaestiones de Veritate.*

———. *Summa Theologiae.*

Arterburn, Stephen, and Jack Felton. *Toxic Faith*. Nashville: Oliver Nelson, 1991.

Augustine. *Confessions*. Book 1, chapter 1. Garden City, NY: Image Books, 1960.

Boehm, James A. "Bishop Ottenweller Determines to Correct Abuses within Local Charismatic Community." *The Steubenville Register* 46, no. 19 (June 21, 1991).

Clark, Peter, Muriel Mooney, and Jo Noetzel. "Report on the Training Course." Privately printed and distributed. Ann Arbor, MI, April 1991.

Clark, Stephen B. *Building Christian Communities*. Notre Dame: Ave Maria Press, 1972.

———. *Covenant Community and Church*. Ann Arbor: Servant Publications, 1992.

———. *Knowing God's Will*. Ann Arbor: Servant Books, 1974.

———. *Man and Woman in Christ*. Ann Arbor: Servant Books, 1980.

———. *Patterns of Christian Community*. Ann Arbor: Servant Books, 1984.

———. *Unordained Elders and Renewal Communities*. New York: Paulist Press, 1976.

Congregation for the Doctrine of the Faith. *The Church Understood as Communion*. Joseph Cardinal Ratzinger, Prefect, and Most Reverend Albert Bovone.

Crumm, David. "The Rise and Fall of a Heavenly Empire." *Detroit Free Press Magazine*, September 20, 1992.

DeCelles, Paul. "For the Record: An Interview with Overall Coordinator Paul DeCelles—Safeguards." *Vine and Branches* 7, no. 3 (April 1991).

———. "For the Record: An Interview with Overall Coordinator Paul DeCelles—The Pastoral Care of Married Women." *Vine and Branches* 5, no. 7 (August 1989).

———. "Going All Out." *Pastoral Renewal* 5, no. 2 (August 1980).

———. "When Is 'Community' Not Community." *New Heaven/New Earth*, July 1985.

Enroth, Ronald M. *Churches That Abuse*. Grand Rapids: Zondervan, 1992.

Ford, Josephine M. *Which Way for Catholic Pentecostals*. New York: Harper & Row, 1976.

Gerosa, Libero. *Charisma und Recht: Kirchenrechtliche Überlegungen zum „Urcharisma" der neuen Vereinigungsformen in der Kirche*. Trier:

Johannes Verlag, 1989.

Hassan, Steven. *Combatting Cult Mind Control.* Rochester, VT: Park Street Press, 1988.

Havel, Václav *Open Letters,* translated by Paul Wilson, London: Faber & Faber, 1991.

John of the Cross. "Ascent of Mount Carmel." In *The Collected Works of St. John of the Cross*, translated by Kieran Kavanaugh and Otilio Rodriguez. Washington, DC: ICS Publications, 2017.

———. "Dark Night of the Soul." In *The Collected Works of St. John of the Cross*, translated by Kieran Kavanaugh and Otilio Rodriguez. Washington, DC: ICS Publications, 2017.

John Paul II. Apostolic Exhortation *Christifideles Laici.*

———. Apostolic Exhortation *Pastores Dabo Vobis.*

———. Encyclical *Redemptor Hominis.*

———. Encyclical *Redemptoris Missio.*

———. "In-Flight Remarks to Journalists." *L'Osservatore Romano*, English edition, February 26, 1992.

Johnson, David, and Jeff VanVonderen. *The Subtle Power of Spiritual Abuse.* Minneapolis: Bethany House, 1991.

LeBar, James. *Cults, Sects and the New Age.* Huntington, IN: OSV Press, 1989.

Leifeld, Wendy. "The Gender Issue, 2." *The National Catholic Register*, May 24, 1992.

Lubac, Henri de. *The Motherhood of the Church.* San Francisco: Ignatius Press, 1982.

McDonnell, Kilian. *The Charismatic Renewal and Ecumenism.* Ann

Arbor: Servant, 1978.

McKenzie, John L. *Dictionary of the Bible*. New York: Macmillan, 1965.

National Conference of Catholic Bishops. *A Pastoral Statement on the Catholic Charismatic Renewal*. Washington, DC, 1989.

O'Connor, Edward D. *The Pentecostal Movement in the Catholic Church*. Notre Dame, IN: Ave Maria Press, 1971.

Paul VI, Encyclical *Humanae Vitae* (Vatican City: Libreria Editrice Vaticana, 1968).

Pius XII. Encyclical *Mystici Corporis*. A.A.S. XXXV.

"Prophecies Given at St. Peter's Basilica during the Closing Eucharist on Pentecost Monday." *New Covenant*, July 1975.

de Robien, Mathilde, "Pourquoi le Vatican ordonne un visite apostolique au sein de la Communauté de l'Emmanuel?", *Aletheia*,. Downloaded 2 November 2025 from https://fr.aleteia.org/2025/10/28/pourquoi-le-vatican-ordonne-une-visite-apostolique-au-sein-de-la-communaute-de-lemmanuel/?utm_medium=email&utm_source=sendgrid&utm_campaign=EM-FR-Newsletter-WeeklySunday-&utm_content=Newsletter&utm_term=20251102.

Ratzinger, Joseph. *Behold the Pierced One*. San Francisco: Ignatius Press, 1986.

———. *The Open Circle: The Meaning of Christian Brotherhood*. New York: Sheed & Ward, 1966.

Reimers, Adrian J. "Covenant Community: A Failed Promise." *Fidelity*, May 1986. Reprinted in *Cultic Studies Journal* 3, no. 1 (Spring-Summer 1986).

———. "More than the Devil's Due." *Cultic Studies Journal* 11, no.

1 (1994).

"St. Gregory the Great on Pastoral Care." *National Catholic Register*, June 14, 1992.

Second Vatican Council. Decree on Ecumenism, *Unitatis Redintegratio.*

———. Decree on the Ministry and Life of Priests, *Presbyterorum Ordinis.*

———. Dogmatic Constitution on Divine Revelation, *Dei Verbum.*

———. Dogmatic Constitution on the Church, *Lumen Gentium.*

———. Constitution on Sacred Liturgy, *Sacrosanctum Concilium.*

———. Decree Concerning the Pastoral Office of Bishops in the Church *Christus Dominus,*

Thigpen, Paul, *Manual for Spiritual Warfare*, Tan Books, Charlotte, NC, 2014

Wojtyła, Karol (John Paul II). *Love and Responsibility*. New York: Farrar, Straus, Giroux, 1981.

———. *The Lublin Lectures/Wykłady Lubelskie*. Lublin: Towarzystwo Tomasza z Akwinu, 2020.

———. *Person and Act*. Washington, DC: The Catholic University of America Press, 2021.

———. "Thomistic Personalism." In *Person and Community*. New York: Peter Lang, 1993.

Yocum, Bruce. "A Response to John Haughey's Paper." In *Theological Reflections on the Charismatic Renewal*, edited by John C. Haughey, 125–29. Ann Arbor: Servant Publications, 1978.

Unpublished Materials

Minutes. "General Council Meeting." August 8–10, 1977.

People of Praise. "Caribbean Outreach." Undated memo.

———. Minutes, various coordinators' meetings.

———. "Pastoral Guidelines."

———. "Principles of Structure and Government of the People of Praise."

———. "The Spirit and Purpose of the People of Praise."

Steve Clark. Memo to Paul DeCelles, Kevin Ranaghan, Ralph Martin, Jim McFadden, and Bruce Yocum. July 18, 1977.

Sword of the Spirit. "Constitution of the Sword of the Spirit." June 1989.

INDEX

ABOUT THE AUTHOR

Adrian J. Reimers is a philosopher who has taught at the University of Notre Dame, Holy Cross College, and the Pontifical University of John Paul II in Kraków. He holds a Ph.D. in Philosophy from the Internationale Akademie für Philosophie and degrees from Notre Dame. Author of eight books including *The Ethos of the Christian Heart* and *Hell and the Mercy of God,* Reimers has written extensively on Catholic philosophy and the thought of John Paul II. A founding member of the People of Praise, he brings both rigor and twelve years of insider experience to this study. He lives in South Bend, Indiana.